From Cattle to Classroom

Evelyn Dando

First published by Busybird Publishing 2024

Copyright © 2024 Evelyn Dando

ISBN
Print: 978-1-923216-28-0

This work is copyright. Apart from any use permitted under the *Copyright Act 1968*, no part of this publication may be reproduced, stored in a retrieval system or transmitted in any form or by any means, electronic, mechanical, photocopying, recording or otherwise, without the prior written permission of Evelyn Dando

The information in this book is based on the author's experiences and opinions. The author and publisher disclaim responsibility for any adverse consequences, which may result from use of the information contained herein. Permission to use any external content has been sought by the author. Any breaches will be rectified in further editions of the book.

Cover Image: Evelyn Dando

Cover design: Busybird Publishing

Layout and typesetting: Busybird Publishing

Busybird Publishing
2/118 Para Road
Montmorency, Victoria
Australia 3094
www.busybird.com.au

To my remarkable children, Wayne, Michelle, and Kevin, and my husbands, Kevin Jackson and Frank Dando.

Contents

The Early Years – My Parents 1
The Bayswater Property – 1945 5
Driving the Cattle 9
Being Sent Away 11
Against the Law 13
Staying with Aunt Eileen 15
Moving the Cattle and Steels Creek 19
School and Steels Creek 23
The Lilydale High School Years 29
The Writing Competition 33
Leaving Life at Steels Creek 36
First Employment 38
Harston Sensitizing Co. 39
Port Arthur 41
Early Married Life in Brunswick – The Fire 43
Tell the Truth 47
Holidays at Burt's in Dingee 49
Our Own First House 50
Britex Metal Products 52
Pigeons at Britex 54
At Reservoir in the 1960s 57
My First School – 1978 61
Unusual Experiences as a Primary Teacher 65

Photos 68

Moving On – Meeting Frank 82
Frank and his School, Education, Soccer Saul, etc. 85
Frank Begins His Own School 88

Zak Arrives	90
My Early Years at FDSA	94
The Strap	96
The Triplets	98
The Trouble with Jet	103
Frank's Recollections	110
The Judo Years	114
Skiing	118
My Art Years	122
Janine	126
AMAHOF	128
My Three Children	131
All on a Handshake – 1996	144
Retirement	148

The Early Years – My Parents

I was born in December 1939, just after World War Two broke out. My father was a farmer and worked on his parents' dairy farm – first in Leongatha, but at the time I was born his family had settled on a mixed market-garden and cattle farm on Scoresby Road, Scoresby. My parents rented a tiny two-bedroom cottage, just off Burwood Highway, from a Mr Braveston.

My earliest memory was when I was about three years old. The cottage we lived in had no power and we had to gather sticks for the fire that my mother cooked on. I had a brother John, a year older, and another brother Ken, a year younger. I was with my brothers gathering sticks one day, when I called out that a stick had jumped up and bitten me on the finger.

My mother was home alone and had to carry me to the main farmhouse about ten minutes away, so they could get a doctor to look at my index finger. I do not remember the details of the consultation, but I now have the scars of two cuts across the first joint of my righthand index finger, where the doctor cut in between the fang-like dots. As there are two parallel one-centimetre-long cuts, the snake obviously had two strikes at me. My mother told me that the advice of the time was to cut the wound and suck the blood out, hopefully taking the poison out with it. She said that apart from being a bit off-colour, I was none the worse for the experience.

In March 1941, my father joined the army. As a farmer, he could have stayed home but he wanted to support his older brother Jim, who had already joined up. He was assigned no. VX51974 in the 2/14th Battalion and set off to Puckapunyal. After training, he was sent off in a boat – first to the Middle East, where they were stationed in Palestine and Syria, and later he trained to go to New Guinea.

My father brought back many mementos of his time in the Middle East, such as velvet cushion covers with golden tassels and a mother-of-pearl brooch with my name in it, bought in Syria, which I still have. I can remember him saying to me, "I bought this mother of pearl for the loveliest girl in the world." I also have his letters from the Middle East written on lightweight Salvation Army airmail paper with their shield in the corner, which were headed "somewhere abroad."

The soldiers in the Middle East were brought back to Australia following the Japanese invasion of Malaysia and the initial landing in New Guinea. They had to train for a very different war in the jungles and were sent to Far North Queensland, around Maroochydore. The soldiers came home for a short leave before departing to support our troops in New Guinea.

As the 2/14 were about to leave, my mother, who didn't want her husband to go overseas again, left him with his three young children so that he became absent without leave for three days. My mother was just getting over the results of the illnesses he had suffered in the Middle East, and was afraid to see him go to New Guinea. He had serious eye problems, with sand-damaged eyes from contact fighting in the Middle East and his blue eyes were still suffering when he returned.

My father, on the other hand, felt a deep duty to be with his battalion and to support his fellow countrymen already defending Australia up in New Guinea. I am not sure whether it was this absence or not, but my father never went with the 2/14 to New Guinea. He joined the Engineers Division and stayed in Australia for the rest of the war years. He was discharged in 1944 and came home to the

30-acre farm that my mother had bought in Bayswater with money she managed from his war payments. The property was along the Dandenong Creek and remained in the family until 1993.

Whilst serving with the 2/14, my father had been offered a job by his sergeant for when he returned after the war. He took up the offer from Charlie Butler at Butler's Brick Works in Brunswick, working very long shifts while the dairy farm slowly fell into disrepair.

When my mother moved onto the property, it contained a large, concreted milking shed with a deep spoon drain to carry away the hosed-out mess. Six cow bails with feeding troughs lined one end of the wall. There was a partition with rails between each bail, which we used to tie up the cow's tails, using the long hair at the end of their tails to make a knot. At the other end of the shed was a large hay shed complete with a McKay Harris grass-harvester and a Sunshine chaff-cutter. Between the house and the milking shed was the dairy – a small building with a small window and concrete floor, complete with a Baltic separator. The farmhouse was a substantial weatherboard, with four rooms, a kitchen, and a back and front veranda.

My mother, Jean, was born in 1907 in Malvern and her father was a stockman or drover. Sadly, her mother died from septicaemia when Jean was only seven, and she and her two younger siblings, Mavis and Jack, had to look out for themselves until my grandfather found a new partner – the "stepmother". Life did not get better, as my mother and her sister had to look after the stepmother's children and do many chores.

Their father was away droving most of the time, so he was not aware of his children's poor treatment. Jack was taken with his father to help with the droving and never went to school at all. Jean and Mavis only managed four years at school at the Oakleigh Convent, but my mother always praised the nuns and said they were responsible for her beautiful handwriting and her good basic arithmetic.

My mother and her sister left home as soon as they could find work. They both found live-in jobs as housekeepers at fourteen years of age. My mother looked after and cooked for a Mrs Parkinson of Parkinson Stoves until she married in 1937 at thirty years of age. During this time, my mother developed rheumatic fever and the doctor said she needed plenty of exercise. She learned dancing and gymnastics from a Miss Alice Uren. She went on to become a member of the Tivoli Eight appearing at the Tivoli in Melbourne.

Jean always valued education and often used to sing one of her many sayings to us:

> We march to our places, with clean hands and faces, and pay
> great attention to all we are told, or else we shall never, be
> happy or clever, for learning is better than silver or gold.

She managed to organise quite a large wedding to my father, and the bridal photos show luxurious bouquets, satin dresses and several attendants.

Many years later, my mother's stepmother, whom my mother always spoke of with respect, said, "I thought Len's children were the worst children in the world, but now I think they must have been the best."

We did not see much of the stepmother – she had left my grandfather and her interests were with her own children.

We did see my father's mother, Grace Tomkins, whom we called Grandma. She was hard-working, even tempered (like my father), and liked by everyone. My maternal grandfather, Len, lived until he was ninety on his block of land in Springvale, but lived out his last year with my mother in Bayswater, in his old railway carriage, which he had moved from Springvale.

The Bayswater Property – 1945

On the farm at Bayswater, which my mother had bought with my father's war payments, my mother was settled and enjoyed her own home. She was very frugal in the purchase of food or clothing. She especially enjoyed going to the Dandenong market and sitting in the round stockyard while the stock auctions took place.

We would travel in the horse-drawn jinker from Bayswater, sitting at her feet while Dolly the pony trotted along. At the market, we would often come across our father's brothers who were farmers, and one brother in particular would not want to recognise us, as we were barefooted and always looked scruffy.

When I was about eight, my mother constantly wore her short, blue rubber boots and carried her small suitcase. Mum would often buy calves or cattle with calves at foot, and my father would milk the cows when he returned from work. Often, we would hold the kerosene hurricane lantern while he milked.

Coming from his parents' dairy farm, my father was a fast and skilful milker. He would wash the cow's milk bag then milk with his hands, putting his head into the cow's flank, with the bucket to catch the milk firmly wedged between his knees. Soon, we could hear the purring of the continuous stream of milk while we minded the cow's tail from swishing into his eyes. All seemed to be done effortlessly.

When my father wanted to make cream to sell, or to make butter, he would set up the Baltic separator. We separated the milk by turning the handle, and a spout poured the milk on one side and the cream on the other. To succeed in using this machine, we had to maintain a steady rhythm for the correct number of revolutions. If this rhythm was not evenly maintained, the milk vat began to shake and milk and cream spattered everywhere. My brother Ken and I found singing the old hymn "Shall we gather at the river" useful to keep up the steady pace.

We would carry a bucket of milk or cream over the paddock and across the drain to our neighbours, the Busches of Waldheim Guest House, about ten minutes away. I would carry the milk while my brother Ken carried the lantern.

My mother used to give us a lot of milk to drink and make her own butter, so we often had bread and milk for a meal. This was made by cutting bread into squares and pouring boiling water onto it. Then a saucer would be pushed into the bowl so the water drained off before milk and a sprinkle of sugar were added. Another lunch idea she had when I first began school, was to spread bread with the dripping that had cooked sausages or rissoles, and sprinkle it with salt and pepper. She never discarded fat – it could always be heated and skimmed off the top. Any leftover fat could be used to light a fire in the morning.

When I started school at Bayswater Primary School, my mother would come up to the school at lunchtimes and bring these dripping sandwiches and a drink of cocoa in a washed sauce-bottle. The cocoa would still be warm. We would sit under a large tree in the grounds of Bayswater Primary School and sometimes the visiting religious instruction lady would sit with us and give us colourful religious texts to keep.

My mother would make a large preserving pan of damson plum jam from the plum tree overhanging the veranda. When it grew mould, we scraped the mould off the top and ate the jam underneath. We did not have a refrigerator, but a Coolgardie safe was used to keep milk and butter. This was a smallish metal safe with perforations to allow airflow.

My mother occasionally bought steak, which she always gave to my father with gravy and mashed potatoes. Rissoles in gravy was a treat for us. She had been a cook, so all of her food was tasty and carefully prepared. On the odd occasion we had sweets, she would make bread and milk puddings and sometimes jelly.

When we went to the grocer in Bayswater, we always dealt with Pegler's General Store on Mountain Highway. The grocer – a Mr Ken Byers – would measure out the sugar with a scoop, weigh it, place it in a brown bag, and fold the top down, then tie it up with string that dangled from a tin suspended from the ceiling of the shop. Sometimes we would buy sixpence of loose broken biscuits – again placed in a brown paper bag after the biscuits were taken from a large tin and weighed. When my sister Marian was born in 1946, my mother used to buy a pound of Swallow and Ariell's milk arrowroot biscuits. She would place one in a saucer, crush it and pour water over it, drain it, add milk, and give it to the baby.

At Bayswater, we were surrounded by orchards, so fruit was readily available. Everyone seemed to have apples and peaches. We had three different types of plums on our property. One day, we took some cherries from one of the large orchards adjacent to our property. It upset our father so much to think we were dishonest that we didn't go to the cherry orchard again.

There was a pine-tree plantation across the creek from our property where a collection of bee hives, consisting of many white boxes, had been placed. My brothers and I decided to try to take one of the frames of honey – but how to get it without being stung? We thought we would just grab one frame and hold it high above our heads, whilst running down the hill as fast as we could. Just as I lifted the lid and grasped the frame, I heard a horse's hooves galloping toward us. We ran faster than we thought possible and managed to cross the creek and find refuge in the bushes and trees on our side of the creek. We loved eating the honeycomb and the honey, and we never did get stung. Sometime later, we returned the frame to near the hives and decided it was not something we wanted to do again.

Dandenong Creek bordered our property – it was lined with willow trees and very pretty. Usually, the creek was not very deep or wide and could be crossed easily. We used to cross it to go to Heathmont Station. My father had placed a hand wire along a large log that had fallen across the water.

One day, I think it was in 1945 when I was six, the creek flooded and water was running over the log. Ken and I thought it would be fun to run along the log, which we could still see below the water. As I tried to walk along the log it became very slippery and I fell into the creek, which had a strong current due to the flood. I can still remember seeing the water at eye level and trying unsuccessfully to scramble back on the log. Luckily, Ken, who was only five, grabbed my hair, pulling me enough for me to reach the log again. When we arrived home dripping wet, my mother thought it was an omen and backed the horse Rainbird, which won the Melbourne Cup that year.

I turned four on 16 December 1943 and began prep the following February at the Bayswater State School about three kilometres away. I loved school and remember my prep teacher, a Miss Canty, in the infant room. My most striking memory was of boys who wore short, lined serge trousers, and the teacher would pull up the trouser leg and, with her hand, slap the naughty child on the upper thigh.

Driving the Cattle

By the time I was in grade four, my parents had fifty-six cows and the thirty-acre Bayswater property could not permanently sustain them so they bought another 100-acre property in Warburton. Then, in 1948, they bought a further property at Steels Creek, near Yarra Glen. There were now five children in the family: my brothers, John and Ken, and I were born before the war, Marian was born in 1946, and Colin was born in 1948. The cattle had to be taken from the Bayswater property and driven to Warburton or Steels Creek to alternate the feed available. These years had a great impact on my life.

My two brothers and I would drive the cattle on foot the twenty-five miles to Steels Creek or the thirty-two miles to Warburton in two days. We would have to run across from one side of the road to the other, waving our sticks, to keep the cattle moving.

On one occasion, in 1950, Ken and I were bringing the cattle from Warburton and had made slow progress. We were just outside of Seville and still a long way from home in Bayswater, when darkness began to fall. Our choice was to bed the cattle on the grass verge on the side of the road or find a paddock. The idea of using the grass verge brought back unpleasant memories of a previous emergency when we had to sleep on the roadside with the cattle and had woken to find a heavy coating of frost covering the huge army greatcoat that was our only shelter.

While we were pondering what to do, a local butcher came past and suggested we try the local football ground because it was fenced and had a gate. It was a Friday night and we had just herded them in and shut the gate, when another local came by and warned us that those cattle had better be gone at daybreak, as the ground was to be used for an important game of football the next day. We were up early and caught the 7 am train from Warburton, back to Seville. We had the cattle well away by the time the footballers realised that all the "mud" was not what it seemed.

Being Sent Away

My mother never seemed to have much energy and was always trying to send us away to live with someone else – anyone really. When my younger brother Ken was born in 1941, I was sent to the Berry Street babies home and stayed for six months, and when my younger sister Marian was born in 1946, Ken and I were both sent to live with a Russian lady – a Mrs Zvikevitch on Mountain Highway, Bayswater.

The cultural changes were startling. She made us sauerkraut, homemade yoghurt and pumpkin soup – all unusual at those times. She would also give us a small glass of stout to "build us up". Despite the strangeness, this woman was very good to us and we always had enough to eat. She owned two brown and white pointer dogs, Pluto and Laddie, whom we came to like very much. When her husband came home a bit under the weather, she would be very cross with him and say, "Get for like dog under table," which used to appeal to our sense of humour. We stayed there for about two months, and for years after she would always look for us coming home from school, call us in, and give us something to eat.

When Mum had the next child, my brother Colin, in 1948, Ken and I were sent to a nurse on Burwood Highway, Lower Ferntree Gully. This lady had other children staying with her, but we didn't know much about them. She was very strict and would make us sit still for an hour each day without moving or speaking. I was a little older than Ken and he would begin to fidget and poke his fingers into a hole in the fabric of the couch. She would then hit his fingers with a stick. At 6 pm each evening she would make us say grace. She would sit at the head of the table and say, "For …" and we would have to complete her version of grace.

What we were saying had little meaning to us, and it seemed to me that we said, "For health and strength and daily bread, we prize thy name thy lord, amen."

If anyone should stumble or giggle, she would become quite fierce and make everyone start again. After this, we would have to eat very quietly and not speak while the serial *Martin's Corner* played on the radio. She used to make our lunch, which she called a healthy "Oslo" lunch, with a brown-bread cheese sandwich and an orange.

We attended the Wantirna South Primary School on Tyner Road at this time, and we always had a hot cocoa drink, supplied by the school at recess. Our older brother John stayed at Grandma's and attended the same school. He always had a sandwich, a piece of fruit, and a piece of cake that we used to envy. We were glad to leave the nurse, although I concede she was fair and we had consistency in our lives.

The property at Bayswater was thirty acres and had the Dandenong Creek running along its boundary (it is now reserved for the Healesville Freeway). The local scout group used to camp along the creek and would fish, although I remember that eels were the most common catch. We used to fish there too, and when we caught the eels, my father would cut around their heads and rub salt on his hands, then peel the skin off. My mother didn't like the look of these eels so my father would clean them, cut them in pieces, dip them in flour, and fry them. We thought they tasted delicious and even my mother had to agree that they were very nice to eat, but she never liked to see them when they were in their slimy, snake-like state.

Against the Law

One night, in about 1949, we heard a knock at the door. My father lit the glass kerosene table lamp and went to see whom it was. A young couple stood there looking a bit lost. They explained that the young man, John, had camped on the creek with the scouts a few years back, and he wondered if he and his girlfriend, Esther, could sleep in the hay shed. My father agreed, but after a few days had passed with the couple still staying in the shed, my mother and father thought they could stay on our property at Steels Creek.

This property had a railway carriage that had been converted into quite a comfortable house, with a wood stove and an open fireplace. The carriage was perched on the side of a hill on bluestone blocks. It had three compartments used as bedrooms and a kitchen sitting area, as well as a pantry room with lots of cupboards. The back door set into the hillside had a small veranda and steps going up to an outside sleepout and further up to a laundry and bathroom. There was also a large shed, a chook run, and a long drop-toilet further still up the hill. The house had a rabbit-proof fence around a yard, which fenced the house, and beyond that there was rough feed for the cattle, and the property was quite timbered, affording the cattle shelter.

Mum decided that the three older children, John, Ken and I, could go with John and Esther. I didn't think this was the optimum arrangement, but Dad and Mum bundled us all into the old Hudson truck Dad had just bought, and we drove up to Steels Creek. After about three weeks trying to control us and failing to have any privacy, they decided to return to the Bayswater property and brought us back with them.

They asked Dad if they could stay until John found a job. They still slept in the hay shed but came into the house to eat. John did get a job at an apple orchard, but on his first day there he came home with a shiny, near-new bicycle. When Dad asked him where he got it, he said another worker had given it to him.

Now my father was not tolerant of anyone taking anything that did not belong to them, so he said that the bike had better go back to its owner the next day. The bike continued to arrive home with John, and although my father never discussed it with us, he must have had some serious suspicions.

We were gathered around the fire in the kitchen one night, when we heard the dogs barking. John put his head on one side and listened, then said to my mum, "That'll be the D's," and sure enough a couple of policemen came to the door and a short while later John, Esther, and the bike were gone and we were sent off to bed.

A month later we found out that my father's suspicions were well founded – John was wanted in New South Wales for a jewel robbery. He was tried, sentenced, and sent to Long Bay jail. They were alright to us children, although there were instances when John would get short-tempered with my two brothers, and with good reason, too. We did not get much guidance or discipline from our parents and we were an unruly trio.

Staying with Aunt Eileen

When I was nine, my mother responded to a request from her half-sister Eileen. Eileen had just remarried and was working at the tramways where she had met her husband, George. She had a daughter, Alberta, from her first husband, Albert, who had died in World War Two. Alberta was three years younger than me. Eileen thought I could live with them and attend the Seventh Day Adventist school in Hawthorn. Mum agreed and Aunt Eileen seemed friendly to me. This was not to last! On the second day at her house, she instructed me on how to brush and plait Alberta's hair and generally keep an eye on her when my aunt was at work. There were other tenants sharing the house. Both Alberta and the tenants were interesting and friendly and I still have a good friendship with Alberta today.

The day I was to attend the new school for my first day, my aunt lost patience with me as I grappled to understand how to tie my tie and fold my socks down the required three turns. At my old school, I had dressed in whatever was available and often had no socks on at all. She began to yell at me and call me names until my fumbling fingers would not respond at all. Just as I thought, *How on earth will I manage?* she walked away angrily. This was my lucky break, as one of the tenants came out of their room and quietly showed me how to arrange the socks then how to tie the tie. I was set to begin my new school.

The Tintern Adventist School was a two-storey brick building on Oxley Road, Hawthorn, and had a large tennis complex at the back with a tennis shed that doubled as a small learning area. It was there we learned the wonders of the Old Testament, with stories about Nebuchadnezzar and the Assyrians.

On the way home from school, as I got off the tram on Riversdale Road, I saw a shiny two-shilling piece on the nature strip amongst the grass. I quickly picked it up and put in my pocket. Alberta asked, "What was that?" and I said very importantly that I had found some money and I would hand it to her mother.

When we got home to the house at 62 Brinsley Road, I handed it to my aunt.

Before I could explain, she demanded, "Where did you steal that from?"

I was taken aback but said, "I found it on the nature strip."

She said, "Don't you tell lies to me, my girl, or I will give you the strap."

I said, "I really did find it."

She replied, "Go straight to your room! I don't like liars."

She waved her brown, leather tramways belt at me, and this was the start of the only time in my life that I felt terror.

The incident upset me very much, as I had never had any reason to tell lies and never had. After this, she spoke sharply to me and threatened me and had me do all the menial tasks in the house. I didn't mind the tasks, but the cold nastiness she displayed and the spectre of the brown leather belt made me want to return home to Bayswater.

After a few weeks, my mother came to visit. Alberta and I were sent out to the yard while the adults talked. After a while, my aunt called me in to the room and my usually very placid mother came over and slapped my face. I was shocked, as I could never remember my mother hitting me.

I asked, "What was that for?"

My mother said, "You have been telling Alberta the facts of life."

I replied, "I don't know any facts of life."

My aunt added, "You have been talking about suspenders to Alberta."

I explained, "The only time I mentioned suspenders to Alberta was when the neighbours' little dog was racing around the house dragging a pair of suspenders, and I called to Alberta to catch the dog and get her mother's suspenders from him."

Still not mollified, they lectured me to never mention these things to a young girl. Alberta was trying to back up my explanation but was waved away, and we were sent outside again. Shortly after, my mother left to catch the train back to Bayswater, but I was not allowed to go with her. I was told, "No, this is the best place. You will continue to go to a good school."

As time went on, I came to be very frightened of Aunt Eileen, who, by that time, seemed to actively dislike me. The tenants and Eileen's husband, George, tried to help me in every way they could when Eileen was not present. I noticed George didn't fare much better than I, and there were many unpleasant shouting matches, but mostly a submissive George would agree saying, "Yes, Eiley. Yes, Eiley."

One weekend, my aunt, uncle, Alberta, and I went by train to Warburton, and Mum and Dad were also there. On the way home, my mother and father got off at Ringwood station to continue on the Bayswater. I begged my mother to let me go home with her and even tried to leave the carriage with them, but I was firmly pushed back and the door shut. As an adult, I reminded my mother of this – it was one of the worst experiences of my life.

Two things happened to end my stay with my aunt. Firstly, I took all my school lessons, including religion, very seriously, and tried to tell my family they should never eat pork. Secondly, it was nearing December and although I had done well academically in grade six, the school said I could not be promoted to form one in the senior school, which was upstairs. I was too young, they said. This came about because my mother had sent me to school when I had just turned four, and the school thought a student who was just turning ten at the end of grade six was too young for secondary school.

My mother had very strong views on education. She had only had four years of schooling herself, and wanted her children to study as long as possible. She also said I was developing very strange ideas on what we should eat. She agreed that I should leave straight away and go back to the rural school in Steels Creek, finish grade six and go on to Lilydale High. Bayswater and the cows were looking good to me! However, it was too late for me to enrol in the high school, as in 1948 the school had to apply and only the best students were accepted – the rest stayed at primary school and completed years seven and eight. I completed year seven then went on to Lilydale High.

Moving the Cattle and Steels Creek

I was ten years of age and considered responsible enough to be left at the house with my two brothers to look after the cows, which were mainly kept at the Steels Creek property. My brothers and I drove the cattle to Steels Creek, with the usual rush from one side of the road to the other, waving our sticks to keep the cows moving. We found that if they didn't move, we could put our sticks over the area on the rear of the cows' back where they had been branded with my father's initials (JT), and the poor cows felt the pain and were guaranteed to keep moving.

On the trip, we would seize any opportunity that presented itself. On one trip, a truck laden with what we thought were soft drinks was inching its way through the cattle. We thought if we drove the cattle directly into the path of the slow-moving truck, it would slow even further and the driver would concentrate on avoiding the cattle. As I was in front, I directed the cattle to obstruct the driver, while my older brother was at the back of the truck, quietly taking a couple of drink bottles. He had a successful raid and soon the driver was on his way, none the wiser.

It was a particularly hot day and we were looking forward to the flavoured drink. To our disgust, the brown bottle contained ale, which to our palettes tasted bitter, and after a few mouthfuls we discarded them. Another bottle that my brother thought was a cherry drink was actually sherry. We didn't mind this, although I knew what it was, and we took the bottle along with us. When we got home, we kept it in an old tank we used to sit in and had a mouthful now and then. The old corrugated tank was also great fun to get inside and roll down the hill with a person inside it running along in it.

Another time, we repeated the truck incident – this time, with real soft drink. We were going up the hill out of Seville and the driver was cursing the cows, who were not moving quickly due to our manoeuvres, while we heisted a couple of drink bottles. The driver just nudged a cow, and the cow responded by giving the front guard of his truck a savage kick with her hoof, producing a large dent. We were unrepentant and thought it was hilarious. We fell about laughing.

Sometimes, when we were driving the cattle, my father would come along on his BSA bantam motorcycle and bring us tea in an old sauce bottle. It would be wrapped up and mostly still warm. On those days, Dad would join us and I would be allowed to go back to get his bike after the cattle had moved on. If there was a slight incline, I would ride the bike without the motor on. I remember one ride near Montrose from the top of Canterbury Road, which was gravel at that time. I was able to ride right down to Colchester Road, and thought that was a great feat. It was certainly better than pushing it.

My father worked long hours in a factory in Kensington, but was with us in the evening when we had to herd the fifty-six cattle onto the verge on Hull Road in Mooroolbark. As darkness was falling, we had to sleep on the grass together, covered with my father's army greatcoat. When we woke in the morning, a thick coating of frost covered us. A nearby farmer's wife must have felt a bit sorry for us, as she brought us some sandwiches and a chocolate drink. The communities were smaller then and we had many kindnesses extended to us throughout our lives.

We also drove the cattle over Springvale Road, Springvale, to where my mum's father lived on an acre of land in a tent. This tent had a bed at one end and a fireplace at the other. It was very rudimentary, with a raw wooden table and fruit packing cases to sit on. Cups had been fashioned out of empty spaghetti tins. The drinking lip was hammered down until it was smooth, and a handle was soldered onto the side. Adjacent to Grandad's place was Whites Common, off Springvale Road, where the cows could graze. They had to be watched, so Ken and I stayed down there, living in the tent with our grandfather.

Droving the cattle from Bayswater to Springvale was a bit hazardous, as there was much more traffic than on the trips to Warburton and Steels Creek. We had to go down Mountain Highway to Burwood Highway and up to Springvale Road. We only did that trip once.

My grandfather was quite elderly, but was kind to me, and at least we had enough to eat. He always called me Wild Rose, and he was often exasperated with my older brother John. He would tap on his wooden table and then tap on my older brother's head and say, "Same thing!" Needless to say, my older brother didn't often visit. He always seemed to be with Mum and it was mostly Ken and I everywhere else. While I was at my grandfather's, he shouted Ken and I a visit to the circus, which was performing at the Springvale township. We thought it was terrific and were absolutely in awe of what we saw.

We mainly took the cattle back to Bayswater to be sold off, or back to Steels Creek for feed. Mum and Dad would arrive with us at Steels Creek – Mum usually driving the jinker and Dad, his motor bike. They would stay a day or so then leave us, as Dad would always be working in a factory, usually doing twelve-hour shifts. They would come with some staple foods like Weet-Bix, milk, cocoa, and honey. They would intend to return in a few days, but always the few days would drag into weeks and we would be left with no food, unless there was a milking cow. Dad also had a small crop of potatoes one year, so we could use those, too.

Milking the cow was a real drama. The milking cow was called Alice. She was a jersey cow and she had very long horns. Alice could be enticed into the cow bail with chaff or a handful of hay, but it didn't mean she wanted you to milk her. She usually had a calf at foot, and I'm sure she thought her calf was the one who should get the milk. After she was lured into the bail with the feed, the trick was to get a rope around her leg so she wouldn't lash out with a wild kick or put her dirty foot in the bucket. You tied a thin rope to the end of the bail, threw it between her legs, then dragged it through with a stick. Then you very confidently lifted the rope up and drew back the leg so it was secure. You would put your shoulder or head into the cow's side while you were doing this, and tie a slip knot around the cow's ankle. The cow was already safely in the bail with the wooden pole across, holding her neck in place.

After that, came the method of getting the cow to let her milk down. I found that my movements had to be very confident, and I gripped the teats firmly whilst squeezing. The other hazard was the cow's tail. Often it would trail across my face, leaving green streaks from the scours she might have got that day, or whip across my face and sting. One method I had to avoid this was to plait the hairy end of the tail and wind it onto a nail at the end of the cow's stall.

Letting the cow out was always easy – first the tail and the leg, then the bail. All was well and I would go off with a couple of litres of foaming milk. We did not have the separator at Steels Creek, but we would strain the milk through a piece of cloth to get rid of any hair or other particles. The milk was rich and sweet, except if the cows had eaten the clover – then we would have to put up with the taste.

School and Steels Creek

We had no clock or radio; we relied on environmental sounds. In the morning, we would hear the timber mill's whistle blowing for work to commence at 8 am. The sound echoed around the mountain. If we were late, we could hear the tooting of the Mansfield bus coming around the hairpin bends down Slide Road, as it came down the Great Divide from Glenburn. We had about three miles to walk to the Steels Creek State School, which was a one-teacher school. Sometimes, we misjudged the time and the teacher, Mr Livingstone, would greet us with, "Good afternoon, have you brought the Herald?"

I was in grade seven, having left the Adventist college in grade six. My brothers always seemed to irritate Mr Livingstone and he would often come out with sarcastic and colourful phrases when they didn't give him the correct spelling or maths answer. His face went purple with rage and he would use such phrases as, "You brilliant bird!" or worse, "You nincompoop!" He would also administer the strap if the occasion arose, and he would try to get my brothers to hold out their hands. They would pull them away just as the strap came down. He would then try to hold their fingertips, and after he had nearly given himself the strap, he would use the strap around the seat of their trousers. If my brothers knew they were likely to get the strap, they would stuff gum leaves into the jodhpur-type trousers they wore.

Mr Livingstone taught from prep to year eight. Students in year seven or eight often taught the preps and I can still remember what I taught. Mr Livingstone put "ba, be, bi, bo, and bu" into columns on the blackboard, and I had to encourage the "bubs" to make words from these beginnings. Mr Livingstone was a very traditional teacher, who taught spelling straight from the spelling list that set out graded spelling from grade three to grade eight. We had to learn twelve words each day by chanting rote style and practising at home, or in my case on the way to school. Tables were taught in a similar rote style.

Steels Creek was a one-room building with a small porch at the entry. The school seldom had more than eighteen students. Hot cocoa drink was made by Mr Livingstone's wife, and given out at morning recess. Senior students would help out.

The only other building in the hamlet was the very tiny post office and telephone exchange, which all local calls had to go through. It was run by Marge Wills and all mail had to be collected from there. All of the time we lived at Steels Creek, we never thought about bushfires – even though our property was at the end of the dirt track, adjacent to the Kinglake National Park.

We became known as a scruffy and unruly lot. One mother said, "If it's not Tomkin's cows, it's their kids." On the whole, we found the neighbours a friendly lot.

Children can be very cruel, and on the way home from school once, my younger brother Ken was held down by two older girls, who bullied and hit him. I was there, but unable to help. Ken was a small, thin child and I remember thinking how horrible those bullies were. At that time, you didn't complain about bullying – you just tried to avoid the situations.

One morning, after a series of late arrivals at school, my brothers and I decided we would skip the morning school session. We had arrived near the school, and seeing the children had already gone in, we retreated to a large blackberry bush about a kilometre up the road. We sat inside the huge bush and I tried to compose an absence note that looked like an adult's writing, hoping it would be believed by the teacher. We suddenly became aware of voices – it was the school going on a nature-study walk. We were caught red handed.

The Steels Creek property was seven miles out of Yarra Glen and bread was delivered two times a week (with the papers) to the local families' round, tank-like letter boxes – but not to us. If we were very hungry, we would eat the insides of the neighbours' bread and leave the crusty shell. On one occasion, we ate a neighbour's pies that had just been delivered. There were a few holiday houses along the track to our place, which was right at the end of the dusty Harvey Road. If we were very hungry, we could slip in through a window and find some food in these houses. In 1990, when I was an adult, we had a school reunion and it was interesting to see some of the old neighbours who said they were aware we didn't have much food, so they didn't make too much of a fuss about our behaviour.

We had some interesting experiences at that school. School sports were held on the farmer's paddocks across the road from the school. Any social occasions were held in Radcliffe's Barn up the road. The postman used to roar up the road at 9.30 every morning in his Burgundy Vanguard, leaving a cloud of dust behind him on the way to the very small wooden shed that was used as a post office and telephone exchange by Marge Wills.

School was often ruled by what was happening in the community. One morning, a farmer called in to let the teacher know he was having his crop dusted that morning. The small plane was crop dusting the nearby paddocks, and it was such a novelty that the whole school of fifteen children walked down to the man's farm to watch the light plane skimming across the paddock with white dust streaming behind. Our teacher pinned a note to the chalkboard to let anyone know where we were.

We learned to be very resourceful at Steels Creek, and one day, as I was coming home from school with Ken, we heard a strange noise. It was coming from somewhere near the old deserted house, which was just down the road from our property, and otherwise the afternoon was eerily quiet. Our cattle had strayed onto this property and were grazing on the grass that once had been an orchard. There was not another house around for about two miles. The sounds, which were like someone thrashing through the bush, were ongoing.

Ken and I made our way around the house to the old rambling garden. A brick path led to a well with rough stones around the opening at the top. The noise became louder. We peered into the well, which was half full of water. A young calf had fallen in. We could hear its hooves clattering against the brick sides of the well, and could see it struggling to keep its head above the water. What could we do?

There was no rope around, but we could see some plain wire dangling from the house paddock. We made a noose with a piece of the fencing wire and lowered it into the well, snaring the calf's head. Ken and I pulled hard on the wire and the calf began to move upwards. With a great effort, we yanked it up and over the rim of the well. By this time, the poor calf had nearly choked, and as we loosened the wire around its neck, it let out great strangling gasps and lay on the ground. About five minutes later it sat up and we breathed a sigh of relief. We felt very proud of our efforts, and often talk about it today.

Snakes were prevalent along our tracks and we thought nothing of trying to kill them if they failed to get out of our way. We would stand at the side of the snake and hit it sharply across the back, just behind its head, with a stick. Looking back, it is a wonder we didn't get bitten. We were never frightened of the bush and bushfires never entered our thoughts. Luckily, there were no fires in our time at Steels Creek.

Often, coming along a bush track on a moonlit night, we would hear the thumping of kangaroos travelling through the bush and hear the "old man" sounds of wombats outside the house at night.

Many years later, after I had just sold the property in 2001, a massive fire swept through on its way to Kinglake and Marysville. The fire cost lives and destroyed townships. A few months later, I drove up to see how the neighbours were coping. The new owners of our property, a young couple, had an earth-moving business with appropriate equipment. They were living in the large shed I had put on the property and had converted it into rough, temporary living quarters. They thought they could build a firebreak and stay, but eventually had to flee and only just escaped with their lives. They said they passed some horrific sights on their way out. Amazingly, although every bit of bush and earth was absolutely burnt, the two large corrugated iron sheds on Mum's property were still in place with hardly a scorch mark on them.

When I tried to drive up to see the next-door neighbours, Ed and Amanda Williams, some months after the fire, I was stopped by some locals who said they didn't want sightseers poking about. I was driving a HiLux with rolls of fencing wire for the neighbours. I had also brought a tray of muffins. Their property, built many years after I had lived there as a child, was about three quarters of a mile from our property. When I arrived, after passing many ruins of burnt-out houses along the way, my neighbours said they couldn't leave their property due to the possibility of looters, and to protect their animals that had survived. They said they were offered an old caravan but when it was being delivered, the man said, "Hell, no. I'm taking this back and giving you our new one."

Later they had a one-room old schoolhouse delivered, which they lived in for the years after the fire. Everything on their property was so burnt that the metal had melted into the earth, and I could see our old property, which we had never been able to see through the trees. Their house was gone but a shed built into the side of the hill was intact. In front of the shed was a large cleared paddock and a dam, where they had some goats and a few cattle. They stayed throughout the fire, as they were worried about their animals.

Recently, I saw them on the TV show *Grand Designs*, constructing an innovative new dwelling, built into the hill with many fireproof features and a soil roof. It resembled a bunker, but also had a glass front looking over the paddock and dam. It had been designed by their architect son. It was a remarkable effort, as they were not young and the wife laid mosaic tiles throughout the new house, down on her hands and knees. Such fortitude!

The Lilydale High School Years

After I finished the seventh grade at Steels Creek, I went on to Lilydale High School, which was the closest secondary school to both Steels Creek and to Warburton, and not far from Bayswater, either. Lilydale High School had a stream of buses collecting children from Healesville, Powelltown, Yarra Glen, Steels Creek, and all the towns on the way to Warburton. I now had a form of transport where I could go to the three properties my parents owned. I could also go to Bayswater by train from Lilydale, although from 1954 Ringwood had a secondary school, and if I lived at home in Bayswater I would have been zoned there.

I enjoyed high school and managed to get there from either Steels Creek, Warburton or Bayswater if I was asked to check on the cows. If I was heading off to the station from the house in Bayswater in the morning, I would often meet my father coming home from work, as he always worked night shift at this time at Cork and Seals in Kensington.

I made new friends at high school and my life began to develop more structure.

The house in Bayswater was in a poor state at this time. My mother, who had always lacked energy, was a hoarder – the house was crowded with boxes and clothes were piled up in heaps. There was no space left on the beds, and if I came home to Bayswater, I had to sleep on piles of clothes. Two rooms were so full of things they could not be entered at all. I did not mind that as, unlike at Steels Creek, there was always food there and my family were very pleasant to be with. No one smoked or drank and my parents were quietly spoken. I did feel embarrassed if any of my school friends wanted to visit. I always managed to discourage them, and if they did arrive, we would always stay outside. If relations visited, they too would have to stay outside, and Mum would take a cup of tea out to them.

I was quite an avid reader and also liked to write letters – often to my mother's sister, Aunt Mavis, who lived in New Zealand. Although we didn't have many books, I would catch the train home to Bayswater from Lilydale and had to change trains at Ringwood. There was a forty-minute wait for the changeover. This was a great opportunity for me. I would visit Wards Newsagency and Bookstore, which was almost adjacent to the Ringwood Station. Inside was a huge supply of books. My favourites were the Enid Blyton series, and through my years twelve and thirteen, I would stand in the book section at the back of the shop and read. I would get so engrossed that sometimes I nearly missed my train. In fact, if it was very suspenseful, I would contrive to miss the train and catch the next one home to Heathmont station. I can well remember *The Adventurous Four*, *The Enchanted Wood*, *The Famous Five*, *The Wishing-Chair*, and *The Secret Seven*. I used to think that when I grew up, I would buy them all. Remarkably, when I turned fourteen, I suddenly lost interest in the genre almost overnight.

Lilydale High was an old weatherboard building in Castella Street, Lilydale. The whole school would meet every Thursday morning in the local Athenaeum Hall for a general assembly and to sing the school song, *Respice Lucem* (Look to the Light), which had been written by Judith Lambert – a year five student. The school had a long, detached building at one end of the schoolground, where home economics and cookery were taught. Wearing a white uniform, the teacher, Miss Schooler, would allocate pairs of students to a stove, sink, and bench, and we would cook a two- or three-course meal and learn how to scrub the wooden chopping boards. The long table would be set and proper etiquette was carried out as the meal was served and eaten. This was a very popular class and only available for forms one and two.

Sport was an important component of school life, both at interschool house sports and competitively with other high schools. I can still remember the individual chants of the houses Tate, Everard, Cummins, and Deakin, with their four colours. The school chant reflected the wide area that the Yarra Valley students were drawn from. It went:

Yarra, Yarra, Warbie, Glen,

Wandin, Woori Yallock.

Come on, rally, Yarra Valley,

Wandin, Woori, Din,

Lilydale High School plays to win!

Lilydale High School never gives in!

Yarra, Yarra, Yarra!

When I was going into form three, new buildings were being built on a new site in Cave Hill Road, which was known as the annexe. These buildings were set in a large expanse of flat grassland, and I finished my last three years there, playing hockey on the rough paddocks.

Before she went to New Zealand in around 1946, my Aunt Mavis left all her magazines, which were mainly the English woman type, in our shed across the drain from the house at Bayswater. She said they had good recipes and sewing patterns in them that she intended to use sometime in the future. I loved to go over there to read the magazines. I could always understand the context of the articles, but could never pronounce the words correctly. I would pronounce words such as economy as "eca nommy".

I can still remember Mary Myriatt's advice columns and the short stories, which were quite chaste by today's standards. I would read about a couple sharing a kiss and then, "She found she was having a baby." I decided kissing needed to be thought about very carefully. In those days, there were no human development lessons. It was presumed that parents provided this personal advice, but in my case, friends at school filled the gaps in my knowledge.

I always interpreted a vertical sign on the electric light poles along Mountain Highway, as "DANCER", which puzzled me. Later I came to realise it was "DANGER", which made much more sense.

The Writing Competition

When I was fourteen and staying at Steels Creek to watch the cattle, I was reading a neighbour's Sun newspaper when I noticed an article advertising a competition. The writer had to be under sixteen and the topic was "My Favourite Holiday." I had our usual supply of Weet-Bix and they had cards in them with a picture on one side and text on the other. The cards in the two boxes I had were about Aboriginal people and their crafts, such as their dug-out canoes and their fishing and hunting activities. I decided to write about what it would be like to have a holiday with the Aboriginal people, and described the places I thought they would take me to and the animals we would meet, and how we would build our own shelters. I wrote my story in one of my school exercise books and posted the page off to them.

We did not subscribe to the Sun or any newspaper – it had only been by chance that I had seen the competition details. A few weeks later, I was at my grandmother's house and an older cousin, Valerie, told me she had seen a story and it looked like my name was on it. She produced the newspaper and read out my story. My mother was present and amazed that I had won the story-writing competition.

I received a free flight in an aeroplane over Melbourne and its suburbs with an airline official to point out Melbourne's attractions. I had to leave from Essendon Airport, and, as was typical, off I went to find my own way. My mother told me to catch the train into the city and then catch the Elizabeth Street tram to Essendon. "Just ask, and anyone will tell you how to get there."

I found my way there and had a very exciting time. They took my photo with other girls who had submitted their stories, published it in the Sun and posted a copy out to our address in Bayswater. I still have a copy of the photo today. Sadly, no one kept a copy of the short story.

Many years later, I contacted the Sun newspaper but they couldn't help. My older son, Wayne, suggested I try the State Library for a copy of the newspaper. Amazingly, with their help, half an hour later I was trawling through their microfiche files and there it was!

Lilydale High School had speech nights and school socials, which all took place in the evenings. My parents never came but always sent me along. In those days, all the teachers and students travelled by train, and transport seemed a lot safer. Travelling to school each day, the teachers would always sit at the end of the carriage together and the students dispersed throughout the carriage. Correct school uniform was expected, with the most contentious issue being the wearing of the school straw hat or beret. Detention was given if either the teacher or the "train captain" sighted a student not wearing their beret in winter or their straw hat in summer. We were expected to wear gloves, too, but I don't recall ever owning a pair.

In year nine, Lilydale High held a social night for the students and I needed a decent dress for the occasion. Apart from the school uniform, my dresses were either too small or very unsuitable. Fortunately, my cousin Valerie, who was older than me and very interested in fashion, generously offered me the pick from her wardrobe. I was very proud to wear a white cotton sateen dress with roses and black foliage on a white background. I cannot remember what shoes I wore, but I was so pleased with the dress that I felt outfitted for the occasion.

At this time, I was painfully shy and did not have good social skills. My years at Lilydale High School, from form seven to form eleven, were very enjoyable ones. I made friends in the junior school and a different group of friends in the senior school. I represented the school in the hockey team as a half back. The sports uniform was a pair of navy Bombay bloomers with a white school shirt, a maroon tie, long maroon woollen socks and lace-up shoes.

I really enjoyed learning French and chemistry and managed to pass my leaving certificate (form eleven). My favourite teachers were Mrs Cartwright and Mr Percy and I can still remember the geography that Mr Nelson worked so hard to impart to us. I found the information on the Mekong Delta, Yangtze Kiang, and the Great Lakes of America quite interesting. However, my school report book says, "Many absences have made it impossible for Evelyn to do her best." I applied to enter the Burwood Teacher's College and was accepted; however, I never enrolled there as my life was about to change dramatically.

Meanwhile, my father bought a Bedford truck with high sides to transport the cattle, so we no longer had to drive the cattle along the roads, which was just as well, as traffic had increased. Transport for my parents was also more efficient – first a utility then a truck was available to them. I no longer was left to look after the cattle, but instead travelled to any of the properties. I was often dispatched to check on the cows and see that they were still alright, or that the fences were not broken.

My brothers were working nearby in Bayswater, having left school as soon as they were fourteen, and, as was usual in those times, they were giving most of their wages to Mum. My sister Marian and brother Colin were still at school, and they were left with the cows at both Warburton and Steels Creek. They were also sent to the dreaded Aunt Eileen. They would ring me and I would get them, but my mother would have a mental block about the cruelty inflicted by her stepsister, and they would be sent back there.

Leaving Life at Steels Creek

When I was seventeen, in 1956, I met my future husband Kevin Jackson, who used to come up on weekends to Steels Creek. He was trying to renovate the dilapidated property next-door with the well the calf had fallen in. We became very friendly and he used to provide food for me and my two younger siblings, Marian and Colin, and, as usual, no parent was living with us, although we saw them quite regularly.

I can remember that Kevin asked me to go down to Albert Park and see the movie *Rock Around the Clock*, which was very popular in 1956. He must have been patient, as I told him I could not leave my brother and sister, who were nine and eleven at the time. So off we went, all four of us to see the picture. Kevin had a Chevrolet coupe and could just fit the two younger children in, but if my fifteen-year-old brother came, he had to be in the boot.

One day, a local stopped us in Steels Creek and asked, "Do you know where Pinnacle Lane is?"

Kevin replied, "No, sorry."

There was a squeaking sound from the back of the car – the boot opened and Ken popped his head out and gave the man directions, then closed the boot leaving the man looking astonished.

Another time, Kevin took me to Luna Park. I did not have a suitable coat to wear, so he took me to his parent's house in Port Melbourne and told me to borrow something from his sister's wardrobe. Just as we were in the queue to go on the Big Dipper ride, we met his sister Lorraine, who was staring at the beige coat I was wearing. She later told me that he had lent something to his last girlfriend, who never returned it.

This arrangement did not continue, however, and in 1957, at seventeen years of age, I married Kevin. My mother was not too pleased about this arrangement, but my future in-laws and their extended family were very friendly and helpful. First, my future sister-in law, Leah, who lived in Fitzroy with her husband and four children, asked me to live with them prior to my marriage, and I found a job. I was unable to enter Burwood Teachers College, as in 1957 only single women could train to be teachers. Even if you were halfway through the course and you married, you had to leave. You could not be a regular teacher, either, if you were married. A married woman could be an infant mistress (sewing teacher) but not a grade teacher. I think it may have been a regulation from after the war, when the primary wage-earner (usually the man) was always given preference when applying for a job.

First Employment

I got my first job at seventeen years of age, as a cost clerk at Davies Coop firm in Carlton. My job was costing the wastage from the uniforms they produced, using paper patterns and weighing usage and wastage.

I got married in July 1957, and after marrying, lived in Coburg in a shared house with the owner. After this, I had a new job working at a laboratory in Coburg where they made all types of food wrappings. I would get the cellophane packets and subject them to extremes of heat and cold in airtight containers and ovens, and test any chemicals that may be expelled from the cellophane, before it was considered safe to use as food wrapping.

I left this work when I was about eight months pregnant. It was not thought proper for pregnant women to work, and as soon as the woman began to "show" she was pregnant, she had to leave. I did not say I was pregnant and I would wear an old whalebone corset, which laced up so it could be pulled tight to avoid any observation. If you were a young married woman at that time, an employer would only consider employing you as a last resort. They knew that it was likely the woman would start a family, so she would not be there for long. There was no effective contraception as we know it today, and what was used was very unreliable.

Harston Sensitizing Co.

I had my first child Wayne just before I turned eighteen, and I was fortunate that my sister-in-law Leah offered to mind him while I worked. I was interviewed for a job as a telephonist/sales assistant at Harston Sensitizing Co. in North Fitzroy. This factory brought in rolls of paper and coated them with chemicals so they could be used for developing prints for plans. It was closely allied with a Dutch firm, Van der Grintens, in Holland.

I had no experience with switchboards, but thought, *How hard can it be*? There were only three incoming lines and about twelve extensions. I said that I would be able to work the switchboard, and they thought I was experienced.

I began there when Wayne was three months old. I soon realised this was not the piece of cake I had assumed. The switchboard was a keys-only type – you held the keys down and rang a handle at the side of the board. Soon enough, the board lit up with calls and I was cutting people off and sending calls to the wrong extensions. I developed a thick skin, as I would often open a key to hear a salesman cursing me. I would put on my most placating voice, apologise, and offer to get the caller straight back. Then I would apologise to them, too, and it wasn't long before I became an expert. I really enjoyed this job and became in charge of the office sales, costing out the invoices, and adding the mandatory 12.5% sales tax onto each invoice. My eight-times-tables became automatic!

I trained a new younger girl, Gaye, to work the switchboard while I did the sales and invoices. As the company grew, I became very friendly with the accounting staff and used to mix outside work socially with Gaye, too. I remember my mother visiting me once at the North Fitzroy office, still in her short, blue gumboots and carrying her small suitcase, looking less than ideal in the circumstances. It was at this visit that I stopped being embarrassed by my mother's appearance and accepted that I was a different person and that was her way. She was quite well spoken, always chose her words carefully and was kind in her own way. I kept in touch periodically with Gaye, and was shocked when I saw her appear on TV in 1996. When I visited her in her new house in Doreen in 2022, she relayed these events to me. She also agreed that I could include them in this memoir.

Port Arthur

Gaye, her husband, and a group of close friends, had planned a trip to Tasmania to celebrate a birthday. They decided to visit Port Arthur and were in the Broad Arrow Café when Martin Bryant arrived. She told me he was quizzing patrons with statements like, "It's a great day, isn't it?" and, "Hey, there's not a lot of Japs about; there are a lot of WASPs though."

Gaye was seated with her back to Bryant and when the group heard loud, explosive sounds, then gun shots. Gaye first thought of a re-enactment of a shooting scene they had witnessed years before at Knotts Berry Farm in the US, with bandits jumping off a train. Gaye's husband John could see Bryant and remembers thinking, *What's a good-looking Aussie kid doing this for?* Then two of their friends were shot and Gaye felt the sting of shrapnel across her back. John felt something like a rope burn strike his forehead.

John dragged Gaye under the table and shooshed her. It had all happened so quickly. Shots seemed to be going off every second. As they lay not moving under the table, they could see their friend's legs not moving, and hoped he was pretending like them.

They stayed still until they heard shots moving away toward the souvenir shop. Gaye had earlier seen a girl going out a wheelchair side-entrance, so they ran past and stepped over bodies, which they have little recollection of seeing. The only reason they believe they were not shot was because of the blood and foreign matter from other victims that had splattered over them.

Once outside, their ordeal was not over. They sought refuge by climbing a huge bank and hiding amongst trees. The gunman was still seeking new victims and was moving around. Other patrons sheltered with them, but they did not feel safe even when the police arrived and shepherded them into a hall. The hall had glass windows and the gunman had not been captured.

This dreadful incident brought about change in Australia's gun laws by then Prime Minister John Howard.

Gaye's health was never the same again.

Early Married Life in Brunswick – The Fire

It was not easy working with a baby in the late 1950s. Society thought mothers ought to be home with their children and the system made it hard. I lived in East Brunswick and I had to travel to my sister-in-law's home in North Fitzroy, which was about three kilometres away. There was a tram going up Nicholson Street, but a pram was not allowed on the tram, so I had to walk. Prams could only go on the tram during the off-peak time after 10 am.

After I had dropped Wayne off at Leah's in Scotchmer Street, North Fitzroy, behind Percy's butcher shop, I had to run back to Barkly Street, near St Georges Road, to Harston's to start work. If it was raining, I would wear a shower cap with a scarf over it and a pair of flat shoes, then when I arrived, I would go into the change room and put on my high heels, do my hair, and touch up my makeup. During this time, I was very lucky as Leah loved Wayne and he was very well looked after.

Another problem I encountered was that my husband wore a uniform to work and I was expected to iron it. I had never used an iron in my life and I made a terrible hash of the collar and most of the rest of the garment. The only time I had pressed anything was my navy school tunic with its three box pleats, and for this, I just placed it carefully under a weight such as a mattress. I could wash the garments, because, both at home and now renting, the laundry consisted of a copper and trough. The copper at home was a large cylindrical copper over a wood fire place. I used the clothes stick to lift up and down any items that needed boiling. The wooden trough was used to wash by hand, and the first couple of buckets of water would be trickling out through the cracks until the wood had "taken up" and no longer leaked. The copper was also used to heat water for the bath. This water had to be bucketed to the bath and everyone in turn would share the water.

Here in East Brunswick, the copper was heated by a gas ring and the trough next door was concrete. Eventually, we got a washing machine with wringers on top. The uniform that I ironed looked terrible and my husband was not at all impressed. He didn't understand that this was a new experience for me, but my sister-in-law came to my rescue and explained first to Kevin then to me how to manage.

We had to share the house in Hickford Street, East Brunswick. We rented a room at the front as a bedroom and a bungalow at the back for a kitchen, which was not too pleasant but was what we could afford at that time. We were saving to purchase something of our own. We rented from a Jewish lady who used to come every Thursday evening (probably because that was pay day) to collect the rent from the three couples who occupied her house.

One Saturday I was at home when the Greek man who also lived at the house was soaking his overalls, which had grease on them. Unfortunately for all of us, he was soaking them in a bucket, in petrol, near the gas ring that was busily heating the water.

I was in the bungalow in the back of the house and quite near the copper, when I heard a loud explosion and could see flames shooting out of the laundry. As I ran out the door, the Greek man shouted to me to put the key onto the outside tap so he could turn on the water. I fumbled with the key but eventually got it on and by then the house was in flames. I ran to the front of the house and got Wayne from his cot. My next-door neighbour, whom I hardly knew, took Wayne into her place and I tried to get our few possessions out onto the front lawn. Passers-by all stopped to help and soon most of the furniture from all three families occupying the house was either on the front lawn or the nature strip, and the fire brigade was in charge of the fire.

The Greek man was taken to hospital, as he had returned inside the house and tried to salvage some possessions in the bedroom closest to the laundry. He spent three months in hospital and we never saw him again. We spent the next few nights at our relatives' home. When we returned to the house, it was obvious that we could not live there again, even though our bungalow wasn't burnt. We spent the day cleaning out ours and the neighbour's refrigerators. It was hot weather and the seals on the fridges had melted. The contents were absolutely putrid, but we cleaned them anyway.

Our next residence was with a Lebanese family in Northcote, where we had a small kitchen with an ice box and again a bungalow. We shared the bathroom with the owners and one other tenant. This arrangement worked well and the other tenant, an older woman, helped me wash the nappies, for which I was very grateful. Wayne was now older and we could get on the tram, without the heavy box-type wicker pram, to Leah's.

Life was very different to that in the country at Steels Creek where I had grown up. I was working full time with a baby and was attending night classes training in shorthand and typing at Zercho's Business College in Melbourne. I enjoyed the typing class with the keyboard covered with a box. My fingers would be under the box and I would look at a keyboard chart on the wall. I soon became a reasonable touch typist – a skill I appreciate even today. I could never get enthusiastic about Pitman's Shorthand, and fortunately shorthand is not required today, with most people using computers, emails, and texts.

My husband was used to an ordered life. Although Kevin was very supportive, I found ironing his work uniform difficult. At Bayswater, there was an old, heavy iron you put in the fire amongst the coals, then when it was hot enough, you lifted the iron out with any type of insulation around the handle. It was then placed in a metal slipper, with clips to fasten it. The slipper had a shiny surface and could iron quite well. Eventually, I was able to make a reasonable job with the uniform, but there were a few wrinkly disasters. Also, for the first time, I had to cope with the effects of alcohol at the end of the week. Kevin worked in a hardware store and the plumbers and builders would meet Friday nights and Saturday afternoons.

About this time, my mother suffered a serious motor accident while my older brother was driving her to Steels Creek. She was in the Healesville Hospital and my father asked me to look after my younger sister and brother. I managed to book my brother on a boat and sent him over to New Zealand to my Aunt Mavis – my mother's sister. She ran a boarding house in Wellington, and while she said she could take Colin, it would not be a suitable place for a girl. She had never married but was an interesting character with a very strong personality.

My sister Marian came to live with me, but this was very difficult as I had only the bungalow, which was divided into a bedroom and kitchenette by a wardrobe. Marian had to have a stretcher in the kitchen, and I can remember putting layers of newspapers under the thin camp mattress to make the bed warm enough.

It became obvious that I was not able to manage a fourteen-year-old as well as a young child and go to work as well, so I made arrangements for her to join a boarding school in Lilydale. Even this was a major project requiring bedding and linen all labelled, as well as buying uniforms and books.

She didn't fit in at all well, and after six months there, declared she couldn't stay. We then tried a convent at Kilmore where she was a boarder and came home on holidays. She still says her knees hurt from kneeling on wooden floors while saying prayers. Marian left school at fourteen years of age, got a job at David Lack's in Melbourne, and lived with our Uncle Jack, my mother's brother, in Ascot Vale.

Tell the Truth

While I was at Harston Sensitizing Co., I got on well with the sales staff. The senior sales man, Mr Dixon, was assigned to the South Melbourne area and had Channel Seven as one of his clients. He told me that he had been discussing a program with them that required members of the public to apply to join the show. It was called *Tell the Truth*. There were three contestants; one was genuine and the other two were imposters. Four panel members would ask probing questions of the contestants and try to guess the genuine one. I had seen the show on TV and said I would be willing to have a go, and in fact went on the show two times about nine months apart.

The first time I went on, I had to be a computer programmer. Although I knew little about computers, which were in their infancy at the time in 1960, the idea was to answer in a convincing manner, allowing for outrageous stories. The genuine computer programmer would have a short, familiarising information session with us. I remember one question from the panel was, "What is the most interesting program you have been involved in?"

I answered that I had been required to enter data from the amount of traffic passing through the Flinders Street Station entrance.

Then I was questioned about how the data was gathered and said with a straight face, "A team of high school students provided a tally sheet for one hour."

The good thing was that the panel members had no idea of the type of contestants or their topic, prior to the beginning of the show.

As the program was introduced, each contestant would stand up and say, "My name is Freda Jones and I am a computer programmer." At the end of the show, the panel would individually vote for the person they thought was the genuine one. We received a cash amount for each vote we received.

I received two votes then had to stand up and say, "My name is Evelyn Jackson and I am a sales clerk at Harston Sensitizing Co."

The next imposter would also stand up and identify themselves. Then the genuine person would say, "My name is Freda Jones and I am the real computer programmer."

The next time I was an imposter, I pretended to be a poodle groomer and the three of us contestants each had a toy poodle sitting on our knee throughout the show. It was quite a bit of fun, but it did have some unforeseen consequences. Because I was a telephone sales clerk, the customers would constantly ask me to provide delivery dates for the plan-printing paper Harston's produced. They would say, "Yes, but can we believe you?"

I remained at Harston's until I was expecting my second child. Again, as soon as I began to "show", I was expected to leave.

Holidays at Burt's in Dingee

During the Christmas and Easter holidays, we would go up through the wheat country to Dingee, which is just north of Bendigo. Kevin's two brothers and their families always joined us. We had many holidays swimming in the irrigation channel, unfortunately with leeches, and plucking wild duck and quail, which the brothers enjoyed shooting in the wheat stubble. We all stayed in Burt's very old, ramshackle, weatherboard house, which he allowed us to use as he had built a newer house on the same property.

One of the hazards of the Mallee was the fierce, red dust storms that covered everything both inside and out, and we never knew what state the old house would be in when we arrived. We also got water from an old well with brick sides and a concrete dome on top with a square opening. We would stand on top of the dome and lower a bucket down on a rope. Sometimes there would be a frog in it, but we would empty that bucket into the well and just get a new bucket of water.

These holidays were always fun, and the young cousins enjoyed each other's company. One year, there was a mouse plague with scores of the tiny creatures scurrying away every time a piece of tin or equipment was moved. Fortunately, the mice seemed to be mainly in the sheds and outside the house. We used to get our milk from the dairy down the road, and would take a billy to the farmer who would ladle the milk from a large vat before the milk tankers arrived to transport it away.

Our Own First House

When I left Harstons, I began to look around to see if we were able to buy our own house. In the late 1950s and early 1960s, it was not as simple as applying for a bank loan for a house. We had been paying into the Heidelberg Building Society and had saved 500 pounds, which enabled us to apply to them for a housing loan. I found a house and land package in Reservoir, on the northern outskirts near to Keon Park. It had unmade roads, with lots of huge pot holes and the drainage was the gutters. The toilets were outside with the pan man coming to replace the full toilets once a week.

The building society would not loan the money if repayments exceeded 25% of the man's wage. The price of the Reservoir house and land was three thousand, seven hundred and fifty pounds, and the building society agreed to lend us three thousand pounds. We could not complete the contract, even though the real estate representative came to our bungalow several times to try to work out an agreement. Kevin flatly refused to sign us up to this "huge debt", even though the builder said he could lend us the 250 pounds we needed.

On the last visit by the estate agent, just as he was leaving, Kevin relented and we signed for our house to be built, with a second mortgage to the builder attached to the title.

A few weeks later, Kevin, his brothers, and our families were out rabbiting and collecting firewood for Kevin's parents. As was usual, these days also became a picnic with a game of family cricket. In the middle of the game, Kevin fell over and there was much shouting. "Get up! You've nearly got him out!"

But Kevin just lay there and no amount of noise moved him.

Eventually we ran over to see what was the matter and Kevin said, "I can't stand. My leg is hurting and I cannot put any weight on it."

The leg didn't look misshapen, but as he was in a lot of pain, his brothers helped him into the car and we proceeded to the Royal Melbourne Hospital. After x-rays and consultations, Kevin was transferred to a ward and I went to see how he was. He was sitting up in bed with a very dirty foot protruding from a plaster cast, which extended from his waist to his toes. He explained that both his fibula and tibia were broken. He had twisted his leg on an uneven piece of ground and was amazed at the amount of damage that had been done. This was a disaster for us, as we were to move into our new house in about a month's time. Apart from the physical limitations, there would be no wages coming in.

We did manage to move in with the help of Kevin's brothers, but money was very tight. We bought congoleum – a cheap type of lino covering – for all floors except the kitchen, for which we paid extra for real linoleum. My aunt in New Zealand made curtains for all the windows and sent these over with a large mat for the lounge. We were able to buy our first refrigerator from Webbs in Caulfield. They came to our house and shone projections of pictures of second-hand refrigerators onto our walls. We could either rent or buy. We bought one with one door and a freezer at the top. This refrigerator went for the next twenty years and even then, it was still working when we sold it on the trading post.

Britex Metal Products

While Kevin was out of work, we were managing on unemployment benefits. I thought about looking for work again, and when the next-door neighbour offered to mind the children, I applied for employment. We had a 1959 Holden and I had my licence by this time. I found a position as office manager at Britex Metal Products in Thomastown. This firm employed twenty-seven men; me; the owner, Neil Bennetts; and a tea lady. The wages were good and the job proved interesting.

The main trade was stainless-steel sinks and laundry troughs. These were easy to take orders for, and all orders were placed over the phone as there were no faxes. The special orders were more complicated. I became used to terms like, "eighteen and twenty gauges of stainless steel", and the properties such as molybdenum, which made the stainless steel more impervious to damage. I had a notebook to copy down and draw instructions, and would draw the order up as the client, usually a hardware store or builder, was giving me measurements.

One day, a client, who often used to order stainless-steel sinks, rang to ask to speak to the manager or sales representative. As I was alone in the office, which I was most of the time, I asked him what it was about. I could tell he was very uncomfortable, but I assured him I was very knowledgeable about all products, even ones to be specifically manufactured. Eventually, he managed to say he wanted to order some urinals. Obviously, he thought this topic was not to be entertained by a woman. He did manage to place his order and he was surprised to hear that I could understand concealed and open sparges, and all the other details.

Another time, a lady rang and said, "Could you make me a gut scraper? I need to have it in stainless steel."

I was quite taken back, but questioned her on what she wanted it for. It seemed she was a small chicken-producer and wanted a claw-like device to scrape the offal out of chickens while dressing them. This time, I asked her to post in a rough drawing so I could discuss it with our factory manager and ring her back.

Pigeons at Britex

Eventually, Kevin was able to return to his work as a driver for La Mode Industries, an American underwear company. They were very good to him, even giving him a lump sum of money on his return.

When La Mode closed, Kevin also got a position at Britex as a driver. One of the peculiarities of this factory was that the owner, Mr Neil Bennetts, was a homing-pigeon enthusiast. Neil had a flock of racing pigeons, as did the majority of the workers at Britex. It almost seemed a prerequisite to being employed there. Some even brought a pigeon in to work and released it with a message to their wives, knowing the pigeon would fly directly home to their loft.

It wasn't long before Kevin, always a handy man, built quite an elaborate pigeon loft in our large backyard in Reservoir. He became a member of the Regent Homing Club and even became their treasurer. The loft was comprised of a large, wire-netted cage complete with perches, and a long landing board in front of the "bobs", which the pigeons had to go through when returning from a flight. This loft was meticulously cleaned every weekend by Kevin, with our cat beside him. Pigeon fanciers do not like cats as a rule, due to their hunting methods, but our cat, Mary, would sit patiently in the loft beside him.

The pigeon fanciers bred their own pigeons, and in the racing season would carefully prepare their birds. First, each one would have their feathers smoothed and their feet cleaned with neatsfoot oil; then they would have a rubber ring placed over their foot next to the numbered aluminium identification breeding ring that had been placed on them at birth. The fanciers would enter each pigeon in their racing book and place the hens on one side of the carrying basket and the cocks on the other side, before taking them to the pigeon club each Thursday night. They would then be taken to the transport that carried pigeons from various union clubs to the release point, which could be up to 900 kilometres away in Burke, NSW. Pigeons were all released together by dropping down the side of the truck. The birds would circle round and round high up, get their bearings, and amazingly fly straight home to their individual lofts. The few that didn't arrive home might have found a wheat field and stopped for a day or so. Those pigeons would not fly next season, and had their necks rung!

When the pigeons arrived on the landing board and went through the bobs, their owner, who had been scanning the skies, would remove the rubber ring and drop it into a special clock to record the time taken to travel from the release point, and the key in this special clock turned. The sealed clock would then be taken to the pigeon clubhouse. Overfly time would be calculated if a loft was further away. As there was an entry fee for each pigeon, there were prizes for each race.

I used to write a weekly report for the Sun newspaper with an account of where the race was from, the winner, and any incidental details of interest. Sometimes my report would be shortened by the editor of the newspaper, but Bill Lawry, the cricketer, and his brother Ern belonged to our club and if they got a place, then that report was usually published in its entirety.

It was interesting that all members of the club were men with one exception – Mavis. Not that women were excluded, but few joined. Keeping pigeons, their entry fees, and food – usually Dunn's peas – was quite expensive, and I notice that these days members often have communal lofts, sharing costs.

Bill Lawry was nicknamed "Pigeon" in the cricketing world because of this interest, and I heard on the radio in the first week of September this year that Bill had won the "produce" race, which can be a distance of 980 kms. When the pigeons arrive after this race, they are very thin and quite feeble, so they are given soft or crumbled-up grain. Occasionally, a pigeon arrives with a sliced-open chest from hitting an electric wire. Pigeon fanciers usually sew their own pigeons, but the one time I saw it happen, the pigeon died soon after.

At Reservoir in the 1960s

There was a good community spirit at Reservoir in the 1960s and 70s. Most sports came from the Keon Park Youth Club. They used the church hall in Dundee Street, although later the council built a large new community hall on Dole Ave, Keon Park. The Youth Club had gymnastics, basketball, judo, football, and cricket clubs to begin with. All of these were run by parents and volunteers. I used to go each week and coach the beam balance of the gymnastic club – from a book! I was also the treasurer of this club until I had my third child in 1971, and my name is on the honour board in the new J & M Lake Hall on Dole Ave, Keon Park. Jack and Margaret Lake were the backbone of the Youth Club at this time and were always on hand to open up and help out.

The success of these clubs was mainly due to affordability, as there was little cost due to the many volunteers and parents. Adult activities were also available and it was here that I joined the Keon Park Basketball Club. A husband offered to coach us and he would take most of the seven of us in his Holden station wagon – there were no seatbelt requirements then. Basketball was new to Victoria and only had one venue – the dog pavilion, where the dogs were judged at the Melbourne Show grounds in Ascot Vale. The court was asphalt and had a downhill slope at one end and an uneven surface. A year later, a stadium in Albert Park and another in Coburg were built with timber floors, which are used along with many others today. It was the era of Lindsay Gaze, especially at Coburg.

Life was busy with work, family, and sport, when we decided to have a further addition to our family. Wayne was now fourteen and Michelle was ten. Having a child was not so easy, as I was now a bit older. When I eventually became pregnant, I kept up my usual activities but disaster struck when I was six months pregnant; I was at work and began to feel very unwell, so left work to go to the local doctor. He examined me and said, "Yes, you are going to have this baby, today! As you are booked in to PANCH hospital, I suggest you ring your husband and go straight there."

As Kevin was working in Moonee Ponds and was a driver, which meant he could be anywhere on the road, I decided to drive myself in my little grey Morris Minor the five miles from Thomastown. I was feeling pretty upset but managed the High Street traffic and the baby was born soon after I arrived.

When Kevin arrived, he asked how I had got there and I remember saying, "Look out the window." And sure enough, there was my little grey Morris Minor all alone in the parking lot.

Baby Michael was perfectly formed but too immature for the treatment that was available those days, and he sadly lived only one day. Although I tried to be pretty stoic, I began to keep the other two children home from school to be with me. Soon, I knew that I would be better being busy. My old boss, Neil, asked me to return and this was the best thing for me, and the children returned to school.

I really wanted to have another child, and became pregnant again the following year. This time I gave up work and all my activities at the youth club. The doctors warned me that I could have a premature birth, so I took extra care, even driving to the grocers and sending Wayne in to carry out what we needed, and sitting on a stool when doing vegetables or dishes.

A much-loved baby, Kevin Junior arrived at just seven months in a private hospital in Brunswick, and after careful monitoring by the paediatrician, he thrived. He had to be fed with a tube and his laboured breathing was alarming, with his little chest going up and down, struggling to breathe. From his birth-weight of 4 pounds 11 ounces, he quickly ballooned to a very chubby baby with a mop of white hair. He was allowed home after seven weeks in hospital. Of course, he was spoiled by all.

In 1973, Wayne, our oldest child, was about to turn sixteen and was in year ten. We thought his marks were not doing too well and that he should get an apprenticeship. No one on either side of our families had a tertiary education, and we thought that going on to university was beyond our circle – it was for people much more talented than us. So, we encouraged Wayne to look for a trade. In fact, in the latter part of year ten, Wayne's academic marks improved quite dramatically. Looking at his report book today shows 80% for English and an average mark of 72% overall. With the knowledge I have today, and knowing that most boys settle at about sixteen and a half, he was certainly well capable of further study.

Nevertheless, as was the custom, Wayne declared he would be keen to be an electrician, and when he applied for an apprenticeship with Johns and Waygood's lifts, Kevin and I attended the interview with him. I think we also signed the indenture papers. Looking back, I can see how important parent expectations are. Wayne, a very quiet person, is a qualified electrical mechanic, but also went on to be a significant scientist and a junior coach for the Australian baseball team, winning the Prime Minister's Award for his contribution to sport.

It was while I was at home with baby Kevin, whom we nicknamed Tiger for a reason no one can remember, that I decided I would return to study. I had achieved form five, or leaving certificate as it was in 1956, so in 1974 I enrolled in English in a Coburg High School night course. I enjoyed the study of novels and sat an external examination in November in the Exhibition Building in Carlton, with long lines of other students. I was quite disappointed to get the mark of 59%, but it was enough for me to gain entry to Melbourne Teachers College – a three-year course. I enrolled there, but also enrolled at Coburg Teachers College, and when I was successful, cancelled the Melbourne placement, as Coburg was closer and parking, easier.

Money was still tight and I was wondering if we could afford me not working, when the Education Department gave me a scholarship. It was the first year that studentships were given out to top year twelve (matriculation) high school students, and also to other student teachers. The scholarship was for 1000 pounds; not great, but still welcome.

My first year at the Coburg Teachers College, it became the State College of Victoria at Coburg, and I found that year quite challenging. The curriculum focused on improving the student teachers' standard of education, and for English we studied American Literature – a subject not taught at primary school. As well as this, we looked at children's literature and I studied the writings of Colin Thiele and wrote a picture book on the life of Bluey the Racing Pigeon. Mathematics began with the topic of "logic" and my first exam on this topic was confronting.

Comparing answers after the exam with other students, I discovered I had only got one correct. Immediately, I made an appointment with Brian Doig – my maths tutor. He calmed me down and explained that I had only made the conclusions of the long problems incorrectly, and as such, gained the mark of sixty-eight percent. With much more confidence, I completed the year with honours and made maths my second major study.

At the end of my first year, the Education Department issued their final studentships. I had received two credits and the rest honours. I was anxiously scouring the the Sun newspaper to see if my name was amongst the names printed, and to my pleasure, there I was. This gave me a reasonable income as my children were listed as dependants, so I signed on to work as a teacher for at least three years after graduating, in return for the studentship income.

My First School – 1978

The first meeting with the principal at Rosebank Primary, a small school close to my home, saw all the staff gathered in the staffroom. The principal welcomed everyone then stated that all teachers needed to have their courses of study and work programs at his office the next week. The courses were an outline of all you were to teach for each subject for the whole year, complete with methods, evaluation, and corrections of students' progress. I was horrified, because I knew what to do but the enormity for a first-year teacher to complete it in just over a week was too much. At home, I examined my three-year contract to see what it entailed and whether I could leave and go back to the comfortable world of office work. Fortunately for me, a friend from another school gave me good advice, "Just say you are unable to complete this in his timeframe and you will need a month or so, and consult with other teachers in your area."

This was sound advice indeed, and the principal apologised for not taking notice that I was the only first year teacher at the meeting. He also said, "To put students onto their reading ability level, just hear them read, and if they make more than four mistakes on the first page, the book is too hard." This was a fairly rough method, with no graded readers, just interest-based books, but it seemed to work. I had a grade three/four and the class next door was a four/five, and we were soon discussing and sharing ideas.

My confidence grew and the following year I was sent to a larger school where teachers worked in groups, which made planning and teaching much easier. The next year, the school of Thomastown West had nearly 1000 students and Thomastown Meadows opened nearby. Half the staff (myself included) was sent to work at this new school, which had very few resources. There were no female staff assigned above grade two, and the principal at Thomastown West decided I should have grade six. I found this a wonderful school and team – for the next four years I taught with a young male teacher, whom I got on well with. We had to decide the school emblem, uniform, sports teams, and school colours.

As there were not a great deal of books at the school, I ordered class sets of the Sun newspaper to be delivered daily, which we read, then had the students make their own newspaper complete with masthead, comics, stories, and sports reports. We had an excursion to the Sun publishing office in Flinders Street, and the Sun provided a book of activities.

The staff in the upper school became very close and supportive of each other, and a group still meets early in the morning of the last day of school each year. After thirty odd years, 2021 is probably the last, as all are now retired and some have moved away. The catalyst for this closeness of staff was largely due to an erratic administration (and that's an understatement!), which continued until we had the wonderful arrival of Will Curtis and Geoff Jones, who were appointed as vice principals a few years later.

I gained study leave on the recommendation of the vice principal and enrolled in a Bachelor of Social Sciences at Latrobe University. I taught three days a week and attended university two days, as well as a night subject in my own time. The study leave was for three years and I studied legal studies and history – a wonderful period in my life.

Also at this time, my Aunt Mavis in New Zealand, whom I had a close relationship with and always corresponded with regularly, left me and my two other siblings a sizeable inheritance. Her letters from Wellington usually began with, "It's blowing a gale here tonight …" – I believe that's very common in Wellington. We were able to pay off our house and never took out a loan for anything else again.

I enjoyed teaching at the Thomastown schools, but in order to gain promotion, I applied to Campbellfield Primary School, where due to study leave, the principal allotted me the specialist position of Physical Education teacher. I took over from the very efficient Christine Powell and the program was all set out for me. I was able to competently carry out the program for the whole school, and taught preps for the first time.

After a dance lesson with the preps, the class was doing a conga line dance back to their classroom when a small, Turkish boy excitedly rushed up to his teacher with a beaming face and said, "Mrs Jackson say I a champion." So rewarding!

After three years, I was able to apply for a new position as a coordinator, having got my AR – "position with responsibility" – and moved closer to home, back to Thomastown West Primary School. I taught grade five and six until I retired in 1995 when my husband Kevin became ill. At the time, Jeff Kennett was offering teachers a package to leave and was transferring teachers out of their schools to areas where they might be needed. He was reducing the number of teachers and although they were not forced to leave, some were sent to areas they did not want to go. Fortunately, I was not one of those teachers relocated. But the next year, I decided to take the package as Kevin was still ill.

I found it difficult to tell my lovely grade six class that I was leaving three quarters of the way through the year. The children were all sitting on the carpet in front of me and I was considering what explanation to give them for why I was leaving – certainly not to take the package. One of my grade six girls exclaimed, "The reason she has to leave is to help look after her new granddaughter."

Children say the most appropriate things! I really loved this grade and although I retired, I still continued my grade's swimming lessons and end of year social preparation.

Sadly, Kevin developed pancreatic cancer and died a year later in 1996. He always supported what I was doing, and one of his last pieces of advice was, "You make sure you get on with your life." I was fifty-six.

After this, I decided to do emergency teaching at a Catholic school. Not being a Catholic, I was unfamiliar with parts of the curriculum, like liturgies at the nearby church. First thing each morning, there would be prayers. I had grade six, so the students were able to guide me and show me the relevant readings. I began to think this start to the day was an excellent way to settle the children down and they were very respectful.

One morning, we were to say prayers for the dead and light candles. After the session, there was candle wax all over the carpet, which I found impossible to remove. I never found out what the cleaner thought.

Another time with this grade six class, we did painting for art. I was quite good at art and had an excellent session. I had also done a calligraphy course, so I asked the class if they would like their names printed on their work in the Gothic style. They were very enthusiastic, but the next day I taught grade two at the same school, and the grade six teacher made her displeasure very evident, saying I should never have made any mark on her students' artwork. I thought it was pretty silly, as the class had enjoyed the session in every way. Nevertheless, when I took the grade two and they finished their maths work, I asked their teacher if it was OK to write their names on their work before I did it. He was very encouraging and the students enjoyed seeing their names written in calligraphy.

Unusual Experiences as a Primary Teacher

I had many interesting experiences teaching that would raise a few eyebrows today. I had a grade three/four in my first year of teaching in 1978. Each week, my twenty-eight students and I would go in the hired commercial bus to the Heidelberg West Pool for swimming lessons given by just myself, until I enlisted the help of a parent. At Campbellfield as sports teacher, I was able to get my bus licence to use a shared bus with two local secondary schools. Again, I would drive each grade to the pool, and sometimes the library teacher could afford the time to come too. Getting the boys to hurry up when dressing was always pressing as they would dawdle and I would call out to them, threatening to come in – of course I never did. Even the girls took so long it was like watching the "Dance of the Seven Veils" as they attempted to keep their towels in place whilst dressing.

At a small school, although I was a grade teacher, I taught all six grades swimming, as I had my Aust Swim qualification. I had a delightful grade three/four with no behaviour problems. The students mainly came from Italian families with a few Middle Eastern ones, too. When I left my grade to take the other grades swimming, the principal would take my grade. One afternoon, I was standing just outside my classroom door and had dismissed my students. As I was glancing across the oval, I noticed a woman with a tall, thick-set man striding purposefully in my direction. As they came closer, I recognised the woman as one of the parents of a student in my grade. The student was a quiet, average child so I was not expecting any problems. As they came up close, the man was standing directly behind the mother, as though guarding her.

The mother said, "I've come because my boy has been being hit by the teacher and he hasn't done anything to deserve it. I won't have my son being hit!"

"I would never hit your son. I would not have any reason to, anyway," I responded.

I could sense she was very upset and nervous, and from past experience, I knew many parents got really worked up if they had to confront or complain to a teacher.

She immediately said, "Oh, I don't mean you. It is the principal when you are not there. If it can't be stopped, I will complain to the regional office".

After some discussion acknowledging her concerns, I said I would have a meeting and get back to her. The man with her was her brother and he began to relax. It was with some trepidation that I asked to see the principal in his office and relayed the complaint to him. He was very quiet and thoughtful, then said the student didn't work well. He never acknowledged hitting the student, but no further incidents occurred.

At another school, I had a grade five class and when we had group activities, no one would want a certain boy in their group. He always wore a green shirt and the odour emanating from him suggested that he and the green shirt never got washed. I had class hygiene lessons explaining all the health and social reasons why everyone needed a regular wash and clean clothes. Nothing changed, and the student still arrived with the green smelly shirt and dirt on his neck. It came to a head one day when the child sitting next to him wanted to move, even though he was his friend.

I said straight out, "You need to have a bath and change your clothes!"

Three days later the boy's father arrived at my door after 3.30 pm. I could smell alcohol on him and he had a very belligerent manner. He said, "You saya my boy stink?"

I quickly gathered my thoughts. How to de-escalate the mood? I said, "I did tell your boy that after he has his bath, he needs to change his clothes."

The father mumbled a few more complaints, but was obviously mollified, then off he went.

I looked up to see my principal standing a short way off. He said he was ready to intervene, if necessary, as this parent had a history of past quarrels. The principal observed that all seemed to be going fairly smoothly. The next day, a clean student arrived without the green shirt and all was well for a week. After this, the green shirt appeared again and the hygiene declined. I never complained again – I just set the boy apart from his mates when necessary.

Another time, our school was very small, so I organised a shared school camp with a neighbouring school. Camps could be very stressful! Whilst on the camp, a grade six girl from the neighbouring school woke me in the middle of the night with stomach pains. I did not know this child, but she assured me her mother always gave her a hot drink with lemon in it. We sat in the hall with her roommates, who had woken up too.

After an hour with no improvement, I had to wake her male teacher and arrange for her to be taken to the local hospital and for him to ring her parents. The country hospital had limited staff and insisted the student be taken to Melbourne. This left the camp two teachers short, so we had to rearrange activities to fill the gap. The two teachers were away for the day, having arranged to meet the parents halfway to Melbourne. We had thought the child might have had appendicitis, but we heard that was not the case and the student was back at school the next week.

Evelyn Tomkins Bayswater Primary 1948, 2nd row, 3rd from left

Len Rigby – Grandfather Len Rigby on his horse Tilly, outside his tent at Springvale, 1951

Kerosene Lamp used in the 1950s

Steels Creek Primary School

Cattle at Steels Creek

Writing Competition, 1954. After having story published in Sun – prize an aeroplane flight. Evelyn in front in cardigan.

1956 Lilydale High hockey team. Evelyn 1st on left, rear row.

Lilydale High Form V Class, 1956. Evelyn: row 2, 1st girl on left.

Lilydale High, 1955

At Steels Creek age 16, 1957.

At Reservoir. Michelle Wayne and Kevin jnr. 1971.

The Blue Bar Flyer.

Bluey and Tiger

Mum and Dad at Ken's wedding 1974.

Wayne Jackson - pitching coach squatting

Wayne's Sports Award from Prime Minister John Howard

Sports coach.

Sports coach – netball.

Michelle and David, 1983

Michelle and her father Kevin 1983.

Wayne, Michelle, Evelyn and Kevin.

FDSA Classroom

F.D.S.A. School Camp, 2012.

Skiing at Mt Buller.

Mush! Dog sledding at Whistler.

Skiing at Whistler, Canada.

F.D.S.A. Staff from 2001-2021. Sam, Evelyn, Paul, Frank, Zak.

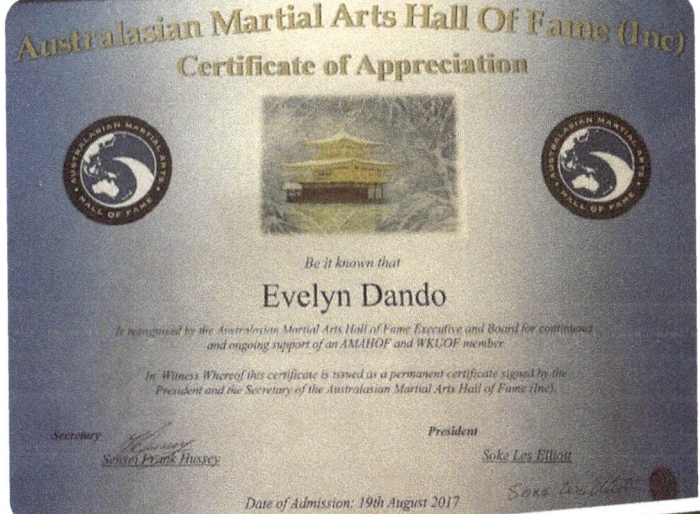

AMAHOF Award

Frank and Evelyn at AMAHOF in Hobart.

Hubcap melted after the 2009 fires.

1st Gully 2009 fires. After the fire 2009 on Steels Creek property

Steels Creek after fires in 2009.

Judo. Frank at Masters Games, age 65.

Bushfire Proof House Roof

Ashford, NSW property. Sold on a handshake.

Retirement from F.D.S.A. Frank and Evelyn, 2021.

Moving On – Meeting Frank

In 1998, two and a half years after I lost Kevin to pancreatic cancer, I met Frank. During this time I tried to be busy – learning Spanish, joining the local square dance group, and training to be an electoral officer with the State Electoral Office. One of Kevin's last pieces of advice to me was, "You are only fifty-six years old. You need to move on with your life." I always remembered those words and tried to do exactly that.

Spanish was not a great success as I kept using French phrases, and square dancing was a lot of fun but I did mess up quite a few sets of "allemande left", etc. I had more success with the electoral office and found the voting process very interesting. I was involved with four elections in Northcote, Broadmeadows, Preston, and Mount Waverley. I became a senior electoral officer, and when I left, I attended a dinner at Parliament House in Spring Street, with a crystal decanter as an appreciation gift. Each election was six weeks of intense work with long hours, but the training was clear and detailed. I enjoyed it even though the Mount Waverley election was close and we had to have a recount under media scrutiny, with scrutineers from all parties hovering over every vote being counted. I hadn't realised that every vote received a payment.

A teacher colleague, Patricia, introduced me to Frank, who was also a teacher, at a dinner party, and he invited me to a barbecue at his home in Ashwood the next week. He lived over the other side of town from Reservoir where I lived, and as I did not know much about him, agreed to go to the barbecue but said I would bring a friend with me.

After such romantic meetings as the Camberwell market and the IMAX Theatre, one afternoon he came up to my family's country property in Warburton. After this, he went overseas for a month skiing in Canada. It was from there that I got to know Frank quite well, as he would ring every afternoon and we had long chats. His interest in education and sport and his obvious intelligence and persistence struck a chord with me. When he returned to Melbourne, I met him at the airport and our relationship became firm – he visited my home and I spent time in Ashwood at his home and school.

Around this time, I had a chance meeting with a young woman at a café who was quite upset and began to tell me how her father had died and her mother brought new boyfriends home who would sit in her father's chair. It became clear to me that Frank used to sit in Kevin's chair, which seemed quite natural. I began to think that my two sons who still lived at home might have similar thoughts. With this in mind, I put the family home up for sale and had a new house built in Kingsbury. Frank and I moved between Ashwood and Kingsbury.

Also at this time, I was asked if I would teach a grade three and four at my old school for six months. The grade teacher had stepped up to vice principal. The school was Thomastown West, one of my favourite schools, which had an excellent principal and traditional structured curriculum. This also meant that I spent more time at my new house, although Frank did visit and even volunteered at my school, sometimes taking gymnastic skills for my grade concert and even cooking Halal sausages for my grade at the end-of-term barbecue.

I completed the six months until the end of the year. The next year I began to spend more time at Frank's and became a member of his staff, supervising the teacher aide.

Frank's school had a major change at this time – his vice principal left suddenly to start his own school, using the same curriculum and model as Frank's and taking some of the new students with him. Frank's son, also a teacher, had a major falling out and left to go to Canada with his Canadian wife.

Frank and his School, Education, Soccer Saul, etc.

The story of how Frank began his school is very interesting. Frank had been educated in the Catholic system. He attended Christian Brothers College with their traditional values, large classes, strict discipline, and focus on extensive reading. When Frank was sixteen, he won the English Literature prize and was awarded a scholarship to complete matriculation at St Kevin's College.

Frank's love of literature meant he was looking forward to adding year twelve literature to his studies. The principal, known as "Soccer Saul", had other ideas. He insisted that Frank enrol in his lethal selection of maths, physics and chemistry, but not English literature. Frank took matters into his own hands. As well as attending the maths/science classes, he secretly read the literature books and presented for the English literature exam along with the maths/sciences subjects, and said, "I passed every subject, very much to my surprise."

Frank chose to enrol at Melbourne Teachers College and began teaching at eighteen years of age. From there, he became a student teacher at Glen Iris Primary School, under the Principal Bill (don't call me Bill) Eddy. Frank explained that along with an infant mistress, who was just as tough as Bill, he was given a crash course in how to manage a big class, which was an art in itself. Frank also described his experiences of school inspectors:

In those days, the inspectors would land on you like a genie out of a bottle, without any warning. Those inspectors were very experienced teachers and had achieved a high standard. By today's standards, they would be classified as outstanding classroom teachers. They would suddenly arrive and drift around absorbing the atmosphere, looking to see whether we student teachers had control of our classes. When they had finished, they would comment and write up a report on "class tone" from which they would work out how useful they thought we were. If they said the class tone was "good" it was time to start looking for another job. Those deemed "very good" or "excellent" knew they had passed inspection and head teachers would be a bit more charitable than usual, deeming you fit to be unleashed into schools.

Frank taught at a variety of primary schools in country and metropolitan areas, and years later, I read a notice in the Sun from someone who had been a student of Frank's at Alamein Primary school. It said, "I remember Mr Dando, his maths, and his rendition of 'Oh Shenandoah'. I think he was also interested in judo."

In 1956, Frank discovered judo. He took a year off and travelled to Japan on a cargo ship. It was not that long after the war had ended and the US occupation was still very visible. Frank was amongst the first Australians to receive a second- degree black belt in judo at the Kodokan in Tokyo. He received many further judo gradings after this while also studying Japanese culture. He also supplemented his income with some non-speaking parts in Japanese films. When asked what parts he played, he said, "A pirate and some foreign devil."

Monash University opened its doors to students in 1961, and it was quite close to where Frank lived. He was given a scholarship by the Education Department and completed a Master's Degree in Education in 1964. This firmed up his philosophy of teaching, and when he was appointed to Clayton Technical School, Frank mixed his theoretical skills, his own experiences at Catholic and state schools, and knowledge of judo instruction, to develop a curriculum for boys who were failing at the Clayton Technical School. Frank had also visited universities in California and studied the Delacatto ideas of movement of the body and academic progress, now allied with perceptual motor program.

At Clayton Technical School, Frank chose to have the lowest ranking students. He devised a curriculum for these students – a curriculum that allowed the boys to become achievers rather than drop outs. That included swimming until the students were dog-tired and happy to behave, and daily judo instruction. His approach to discipline and routine soon convinced him that the state education system was not designed to optimise these boys' learning opportunities.

With a very innovative plan, Frank asked his technical school principal if he could take a group of low achievers in the hall behind the Clayton swimming pool, and improve their swimming and judo skills as well as providing intensive English and maths skills. Frank already possessed a seventh-dan judo qualification and had obtained his Bronze Medallion and Surf Life Saving certificate. He was also a competent skier and skin diver.

His program became so successful that the local municipal council and the Minister of Education became interested. Letters to then Minister Lindsay Thompson, and Director of Technical Schools, Mr Watts, along with responses from Oakleigh Council and the Clayton Technical School principal showed strong support for Frank's initiatives. They provided a cottage, known then as the Annexe, with two other staff members. Frank's method was achieving great results!

Frank Begins His Own School

When the Education Department decided to close the technical schools, Frank chose to open his own school using the judo dojo behind his house in Ashwood as a classroom.

In 1980, the Ashwood Boys School (later renamed Frank Dando Sports Academy) opened with a new curriculum that emphasised English, maths, and physical education. The boys who enrolled had behaviour and self-esteem problems. Swimming, judo, gymnastics, and camps played a major part in the curriculum. It wasn't long before Frank's personality, intellect, and energy came to the fore. Frank appointed the right kind of teachers and the school flourished. He realised that the kind of teaching would have to change. As an example, if a boy were to be disciplined, it would be by doing push-ups, swimming lengths, or doing maths exercises. Occasionally the strap would be given. The boys went on bush and skiing camps. Half of the curriculum was physical activity at a high level of intensity, so it was a relief for many to get back to the books. Activities extended to surfing, scuba diving, skiing, and horse riding.

The focus has remained on providing a supportive, predictable, integrated educational environment with intensive physical activity to engender self-respect and a sense of achievement and resilience in the boys. The boys are learning the curriculum as a part of life and not as something only associated with the classroom.

In 2000, when the two senior teachers left, the school began to operate with Frank, me, a registered teacher, and Graeme – a teacher's aide.

Frank needed some qualified staff!

Zak Arrives

One afternoon, there was a knock at the door of our home in Ashwood, and there stood Zak – a fit, energetic man of thirty years. He explained that he had just graduated from the Catholic University with a Bachelor of Education. He was also an exercise physiologist and a noted martial arts athlete. He also said he had his surf lifesaving certificate, so he seemed the perfect teacher for Frank's school.

Frank and I looked at each other and wondered if he was some sort of stooge sent by our opposition. Just as we were considering Zak, Frank's best friend Bob Todd walked through the door. Bob, a retired teacher, was on the Victorian Martial Arts and Combat board. He greeted Zak straight away and said, "What are you doing here?" Obviously he knew Zak well and soon corroborated Zak's story. Frank was delighted to offer Zak the position for one year to see how he went.

Zak began with pure enthusiasm; his control of students was remarkable – they loved his energy, jokes, and poetry. In fact, he seemed to be handmade for teaching this group of boys who had failed in mainstream schools. The main difference he made was building up a positive attitude in the school. Boys began to respect themselves, their mates, and the school. Students were known to arrive at the school with their head down and an attitude that seemed to say, "Not another school my mum is dragging me to."

They would leave after an interview with us first, then Zak, and they would be smiling, shaking his hand, and, on the odd occasion, giving him a hug. They could see this was not your ordinary school!

So began Zak's teaching career. Frank's knowledge of literature, English, and history was encyclopaedic and he had an old-world presence. Zak was keen to learn and improve his knowledge, and he participated in many practical curriculum ideas. Frank encouraged and assisted Zak to complete a Master's Degree in Special Education based on the effectiveness of Frank's school. Frank tempered Zak's enthusiasm on the student's adventurous activities with his quote, "Remember, when things go wrong, you have to have a good story for the coroner."

Zak never forgot this stark reminder. Outdoor activities were planned with a degree of risk taking – necessary for teenage boys – such as swimming in the ocean in a rip, or abseiling down Camel's Hump at Woodend; they required careful planning and preparation.

Zak was also very charismatic and entertaining. On one camp, the students were inside due to the weather and Zak entertained them by telling vivid stories of the Arabian Nights. Such was his personality. When Zak was in charge, he always managed with confidence and Frank never had any doubts.

Zak brought his friend Paul, a registered teacher, to the school, and he worked three days each week to start, then moved to four days teaching, which he continues to do today. Paul is an exceptional maths teacher – he has the respect of all students and excellent control. He also has a strong work ethic, is a martial arts master, and showed initiative.

Zak also brought another martial arts friend to the school as a teacher's aide. Sam was a boxing enthusiast and a motor mechanic, and as a teacher's aide was the best you could employ.

For the following twenty years, the excellent team of Frank, Zak, Paul, Sam, and I ran the school.

It was important that all had the same understanding of the school and its culture. With Zak's positive energy, the school was always a vibrant place. The school developed a more structured approach. I brought my long experience as a teacher and ideas in developing school curriculum. Reading was paramount to Frank's curriculum, but rather than reading individual books, sets of literature books were carefully selected (all read first by me) to suit student's abilities and interests. The students discussed their books in their ability groups; Sam's group, being the lowest, developed students who had never read a book before. We employed individual English cards using SRA, which measured comprehension and use of English. Mathematics had always been done using the sheets Frank had planned and written out himself, specifically to build the basics that students had failed in, especially times tables and subtraction.

Subtraction, using the more modern approved decomposition method, presented as the most common basic failing that new students showed in maths. As the students were now teenagers, Frank went back to teaching subtraction the old-fashioned way of equal addition, putting "one to the top and one to the bottom," which they grasped almost straight away.

As well as Frank's prepared sheets, I bought "Quest" sets of maths books, reflecting the curriculum standards in years eight, nine, and ten. New students with poor maths still went through Frank's sheets first.

Frank would greet each student on entrance in the morning, and often when they were leaving, with a quick tables quiz. He had also devised a set of "mation tables" listing all the most difficult tables. These were limited to ten or twelve tables, and he would have them on a sheet for the students to rote learn. He knew it was not necessary to teach older students two-, ten-, or eleven-times tables.

I organised a yearly dedicated roll of student's attendance, instead of just checking the daily swimming pool attendance sheet. Having some office experience from my pre-teaching days, I was able to set up a cash-flow bookkeeping system and run the office grant applications, student travel allowances, and many reports. We successfully passed all government audits and many changing government requirements. Frank's main concerns were teaching and attending to behaviour problems, some of which incurred legal summons or custody disputes. His bookkeeping method was to tear out all the cheque butts, paste them onto a piece of paper, and despatch them to the accountant.

My Early Years at FDSA

In 2001, I officially joined the staff and it was also the year I married Frank. At this time, the school consisted of twenty-seven students and was operating at the back of Frank's house in his dojo, in Ashwood. A dojo is built for judo instruction and is like a gymnasium with a red and green, soft canvas floor. Chairs and tables for academic instruction were slotted into a specially constructed wall. The tables could be set up by the teenage students after the physical program, and just as quickly folded away when the larger area was needed.

The students had all failed in the mainstream system, mainly because of behaviour, school refusal, bullying, or lack of interest. They worked in small ability groups. All students had normal IQs as tested by the school psychologist, and some were very bright. The system was harsh but successful and the students thrived and were proud to be there. I found the students all interesting and their behaviour toward me was very respectful. I was fortunate to have a strong group of colleagues supporting me, and, of course, they knew I was Frank's wife. To have students really giving their best effort, especially writing about their activities, was very rewarding.

One evening, when I hadn't been there very long, I answered an interesting telephone call that went:

"Hello, can I speak to Frank?"

"Sorry, he isn't here at present. Can I help you?"

"I just wanted to thank Frank for his encouragement and insisting I read books and improve my English. I still have the book *Master and Commander*, by Patrick O'Brian, he gave to me when I left. I am studying English at the present."

"That's great. What are you hoping to do with it?"

"Well, I am doing it for my VCE."

"What school are you doing that at?"

"Well, of course, I am in prison."

Managing to get my thoughts together, I went on to ask him what he might do after VCE, and we had a pleasant conversation. I never bothered to ask him why he was there.

After I had been teaching there a few years, I received another phone call from a parent of a fifteen-year-old student whom I had in my English class. The mother rang at 9.30 in the evening. She told me that she was exercising her son in the garage – he had been giving her a lot of trouble.

I said that exercising was quite a good idea, but not that late at night.

She wanted to know if she could invite another student to join her, as it might help his behaviour as well.

I said it was too late at night and that too much exercise just before sleep would probably not be helpful.

She then said, "I didn't say *exercising* him. I am *exorcising* him."

I was absolutely flabbergasted and certainly was not going to recommend the student she suggested, nor any other student. We never had any further discussion on that topic.

The Strap

On one occasion, in 2001, Frank gave a new student the strap, which was allowed at that time but banned later. The student's parents brought a complaint against Frank because of his use of the strap. The Registered Schools Board visited to see for themselves.

Every student and their parents attended the meeting, and parents gave testimonies as to the effectiveness of the school. An ex-student, Danny, outlined his life before and after attending the school, which made a strong impact. It brought tears to the eyes of the adults attending.

The conclusion of the meeting by the Registered Schools Board was that punishment should be consistent with using a one-metre cane instead of the strap that Frank had used. The strap looked more like a piece of rubber hose. Being fairly new to the school, I found their edict to use a cane quite confronting. Nevertheless, I was dispatched to a store in Bayswater to buy the cane. When the sales assistant asked what I wanted the cane for, I mumbled something unintelligible, not feeling that I could say that it was for punishing students. There was even a precedent in a court case where corporal punishment was justified if given with appropriate consideration. So, case law supported Frank's action.

The novel *The Slap,* by Christos Tsiolkas, was written in 2008. The book presents the viewpoints of eight characters and focuses on their reactions when a neighbour slaps a boy at a suburban barbecue. The book stirred significant debate and examines the social mores of the time.

The mood of the community was changing and there was a swing against corporal punishment; not many schools were open to admitting they still used it, and corporal punishment was banned in all government schools in 1986 and in all independent schools in 2006, including ours.

Surprisingly, discipline at our school was still effective using a credit system. The students could earn credit points and use them to buy out of some activities or good behaviour could contribute toward interesting excursions on Friday afternoons. One of these interesting excursions was visiting the thousand steps in Tremont, near Ferntree Gully, although some may not find arduously running up and down these steps too pleasurable.

Some newer individual punishment would also involve push-ups or sitting on the wall. Sitting on the wall was sitting against the wall with no chair – said to improve thigh muscles! I often observed students doing these push-ups with no complaints and they accepted why they had to do them. I felt more sorry for the parents who waited patiently for their child to be dismissed, as many had travelled long distances. Other more interesting activities were abseiling in Woodend, horse-riding, tubing the Yarra in Warburton, a camp each term, learning to ski at Mount Hotham, bushwalking, or canoeing.

The Triplets

One day, Frank was reading the Sun when a story caught his eye and he read it out to me. A mother had told her story about her three children to the editor. The boys were triplets and had been diagnosed with ADHD (Attention-deficit/hyperactivity disorder). They had been enrolled at a local high school while they were in year six at their primary school. As the end of year six approached, the high school suddenly found they did not have any more vacancies. The mother didn't know where she could go. She recognised that three children with ADHD could be a problem in any high school. What could she do?

Frank decided to contact her and asked her to bring the children along to our school. He said he would give each child a week's trial separately, and if they could cope, he was willing to enrol them.

Carolyn, the mother, gives this account of her experience:

> I wrote to the Herald Sun newspaper telling them of my plight. The next day they ran a story about us. At 10.00 am my phone rang.
>
> "Hi Carolyn," said the gruff voice at the other end of the phone. "This is Frank Dando. Are you the lady in the newspaper? I think we might have a school for your boys."

After briefly explaining his school to me, I made an appointment for an interview that afternoon. After I hung up the phone, I googled the Frank Dando Sports Academy (FDSA) and found it is a small, independent school offering a specialised program for boys like mine. It is run by Frank Dando and operates at the rear of his private address in Ashwood, Melbourne. From the information I read on the website, I estimated Frank had been teaching for sixty-four years. That would have to make him close to eighty. My curiosity heightened.

After arriving for my appointment, I rang the front doorbell and was greeted by a white-haired gentleman who introduced himself to me with a vigorous handshake.

"Hi, Carolyn. I'm Frank. Come in."

His hair colour was the only hint to his age – there was nothing elderly about Frank. He was wearing the school tracksuit and looked like a ball of muscle and at least twenty years younger than I imagined.

Frank ushered me through to his kitchen and introduced me to his wife, Evelyn, who also works at the school as a teacher. We chatted over the dilemma I was facing with my boys, and their specific learning difficulties. I briefly met the other staff – Zak, Sam, and Paul, all of whom are not only teaching the boys maths and English, but are also expert sportsmen.

Frank explained the format of a standard school day, which consists of one hour of each of the following, in this order:

◊

- ◊ Intense physical exercise such as judo or boxing to expel excess energy and induce better concentration

- ◊ English – using SRA (Science Research Association) – the levels in this program increase in small increments to assist poor readers

- ◊ Swimming at the local pool (travelling in the school's own bus) for stroke development or laps of the pool

- ◊ Maths.

There are no breaks such as recess or lunch. The boys eat any time they are hungry, but there are very strict rules about food – it must be healthy. No junk food, including muesli bars and packaged foods. Unacceptable foods brought to the school will be thrown in the bin!

The rigid environment also applies to the work ethic and expectations of behaviour. The school operates four camps each year in which they deliberately address the issues of adolescent risk taking in a safe, controlled environment. The theory is that the type of boy who attends the school is usually one who, without direction, will find their own risks and thrills if not otherwise challenged. The camps offer challenges such as horse riding, canoeing, abseiling, survival camp (carrying own gear, cooking etc.), snow skiing, and surf lifesaving (including Bronze Medallion). Whilst these activities all sound like heaps of fun (they are!), they also provide opportunities for boys to face and conquer fears – it's scary to abseil down a sheer cliff-face or learn how to swim out of a rip at Cape Woolamai in two-metre surf. The boys' self-esteem soars with these victories.

Carolyn said the school sounded too good to be true and she almost wanted to enrol herself! Her triplets began the following year and despite the boot-camp-type approach, they loved it.

Around this time, a fiery red-headed boy decided to bring a knife to school. I don't know whether he was "pissed off" with Zak or simply going to show the knife he was bringing to the survival camp. He was quite a large, solid student who had been expelled from his last school for hitting a teacher. He dramatically produced the knife, much to the interest of the other students.

Frank just happened to be walking down the stairs at the time, saw the knife, and casually kicked it out of Tom's hand before Tom knew what had hit him.

"Well, that's got rid of the knife," said Frank as he casually walked across the room. Then he told everyone to get back to work.

The triplets were very athletic and became fixated on swimming and judo. All three hold the school record for swimming eighty laps (four kilometres) in one hour.

With Frank's expert coaching and the triplet's application, they all achieved a high degree of skill in judo. They competed in school sports, became the Victorian Junior Champions, and went on to compete in the Australian Judo Tournament in Wollongong, which Frank and I attended. Being identical and the same weight, they often fought each other in a final.

Once the umpire was scratching his head, not knowing which triplet's name to say had won the fight. The umpire had to resort to a video recording of the fight! After this, it became necessary to wear different-coloured belts.

Once the boys left FDSA, they lost interest in judo, but in 2024, after enduring some challenging changes in employment, I learned they had joined the Monash Judo Club and were channelling their energies into it again.

I knew the boys were very difficult socially outside of school, but I always found them to be very interesting, engaged, and polite to me, and, indeed, to all of the staff. In all the time I was connected with them, I had to ask them which triplet they were. Today, they can be individually recognised by their tattoos. They have also returned to the school to give a talk to the current students and have matured considerably, to finally triumph over adversity. Their mother Carolyn Angelin has written two books, *ADHD to the Power of Three* and *ADHD to the Power of Three – The Teenage Years*, about coping with triplets, their activities and how she managed.

The Trouble with Jet

This is a whimsical, piquant account of a teenage student, which most readers will resonate with, written by a parent who wanted his son enrolled the following year:

> Perhaps six weeks after my twelve-year-old son started at Frank Dando's Sports Academy, he answered one of my entirely reasonable requests with the previously unheard "round these desolate parts" two-word reply, "Yes, Dad."
>
> What was even more startling was that he then repeated this miraculous phrase when I asked him to do other things, and was actually following my instructions with action! And all without seventeen miles of whining, the usual ridiculous pantomime of stalling, or angrily scooting off on his bug-out bicycle.
>
> To a far lesser degree, Jet still does dabble in some pre-Frank, Zak, Paul, and Sam behaviour, but he's now almost manageable and without the need for a lasso rope and horse corral. And here's the rub.
>
> Unsurprisingly, needless conflict with my son is often debilitating and heartbreaking, almost literally. The irony is

that Jet is better in many ways than I ever was at twelve. And I know if he wants to, he can be much more of a grown man than I am now.

At primary school, Jet was much liked by his thoughtful, caring, and thus often-exasperated and in-tears teachers. Though due not just to his often-engaging personality, Jet ironically had and still does have many wonderful and usually top student friends. Often contributing great things in his class, especially in discussions, Jet was perhaps that rare thing of a student voicing an original, individual, and coherent opinion.

Despite this and the school's many patient efforts, all of Jet's comic to tragic antics were and are mostly of his own making. Usually, the only disruptive boy in his class and the only kid to run out of his school more than a few times in a red-faced fit for no apparent reason, he was regularly the subject of "What do we try next?" teacher round-tables. They usually concluded that they had no apparent options left, except perhaps bolstering themselves with sedatives in the morning and martinis in the afternoon.

Jet, hiding behind his long hair in silence after some meaningless and inexplicable eruption, was a common and recurrent theme and the subject of many a daytime telephone call, often resulting in me having to come to the school and retrieve said sullen enigma.

Please note that Jet is no delinquent and has never engaged in any illicit or criminal activity, because that's not his character and he doesn't have the government funding. Jet is not a crowd follower and is content in his own company. He has a great sense of humour and is often imaginative, bright, and creative. He enjoys cycling, swimming, surfing, and boxing, and is quite theatrical. He's a lovely boy.

So, why is Jet at Frank's?

Because Jet was not always that much-loved creature and laughter-producing lad, but too often for my tolerance of chronic recurring migraines, could be a negligent, almost randomly destructive one, especially to his own learning and at home. Was this a mixture of his tiredness, boredom, and stress? It was certainly mine. I guess partly, but I don't really know. As I have discovered, he was not such a unique case.

I DO want a school that acknowledges that boys are different to girls and treats boys accordingly – not like some inexplicable misfits who need to conform to what is actually more girl orientated, as per current, popular ideological delusion. But then there's so much of it about.

And I won't allow Jet to be like over 40% of Australian's who are so functionally illiterate that they can't read, write, or comprehend a full paragraph of instructions – revealing the failure of an education system that spent decades rejecting the long-proven phonics method, while keeping corduroy jackets with leather patched elbows.

But I digress.

Jet is at Frank's not just because daily beatings with bamboo would be exhausting and child chimney sweeps are outlawed, but because Jet's pre-Frank response to every other method known to those grimly clinging to their own sanity, was too often a big fat zero and a loud, "Shove it."

Jet is at Frank's because Jet LISTENS to what Frank, Zak, Paul, and Sam say the first time, AND doesn't argue! AND then he amazingly puts what he's learned into action, all while often relaying their much-admired advice to me.

Jet is at Frank's because what he's doing there makes sense for him and it works. It didn't matter at all that sometimes what I said incredibly made some shred of sense. Jet didn't much listen to me, or his mother, or his grandfather.

Jet needs the regular and reinforcing example, instruction, guidance, and influence provided by these strong, thoughtful, experienced, and qualified great men and Frank's wonderful wife and administrator Evelyn, all of whom UNDERSTAND boys. Myself, I barely understand hamsters.

Post Frank, Jet is no longer so "inert" per se, but can verbally express himself far better than before.

The KEY, I believe, to Frank's method is that it's stripped down to fundamentals of mental discipline and physical fitness, mathematics, English, and reading, and more suited to what many boys like Jet can handle. PLUS, boys actually ENJOY what they do there and take pride in their achievements, while spending no time on distractions but only on essentials. Academically, Jet was falling rapidly behind and he barely passed a grudging year or two when he probably shouldn't have.

I don't want Jet to ever start each school day as just another unfit, untucked-shirt and tie-askew, listless teen, sugar and processed-food diet bursting out of their pores in a school where the same land-fill-ready ersatz food is on sale, or where discipline means endlessly tedious "negotiation."

Trying to penetrate easily irked iPod oblivion, like some dystopian sci-fi nightmare come true, is the exact opposite of Frank's Academy, where there is virtually no addictive technology. Choices have clear consequences and one can get a richly deserved ass-kicking. This alone helps me sleep at night!

The result of Jet ending his partly begun and eventually long journey at Frank's now, would be entirely predictable and unpleasant to say the least. For the last several years, many weekends were one long argument in a futile attempt to get Jet to fill almost any responsibility, school work, or to modify his behaviour – or, we just had to totally ignore him as far as possible because hiding overseas would be cruel.

Jet was rather unfit compared to now, and often mind-bendingly lazy, which is a large part, I believe, of why he was alarmingly stubborn and usually for all the entirely wrong things. Sometimes appallingly and explosively rude, routinely uncooperative, obsessed with pointless wasteful behaviour (even physically fighting with us), he could be wilfully obtuse and perverse in many of his choices, told some ridiculous lies, and made sustained efforts at most anything that avoided effort. I saw a future in the public service.

Before Frank, Jet would regularly reduce his mother to tears of rage and despair, and me to my general state of shouting and incompetence. Sure, there was a negative side, too.

If we were in America, which is about as far as we could get away from Jet, I would have put him in either a military college or a working ranch, and on which side of the electric wire fence I can't say. The only choice available to us here was fortunately a pretty good one, and that was the Academy.

The alternative was that no matter his charms, creative spirit, and his playful kindness to his small sister, we were very close to no longer being able to tolerate our own son, except as some kind of glass-jar-residing Exhibit A.

At almost every school, Jet was that loveable yet suddenly awkwardly difficult kid – though often lively and able to focus ferociously on singular projects. He could be just as randomly uninterested, oblivious, bored, restless, and painful to everyone else around him, leaving everyone concerned and perplexed. For all I know, the whole thing may be my fault, though I doubt it, and either way, that doesn't help Jet.

We have presented him with many positive opportunities, which neither I nor my wife could ever have dreamed of as typically clueless kids or typically clueless adults. And far too often, our efforts were to no avail.

Curiously, Jet was very much looking forward to going to high school – until he got there and found it rather lacklustre and unfocused and, it was to him, rather irrelevant. He also found, to his surprise, that his poopy behaviour did not fill people with glee and applause.

So, Jet was going to another more regular, pleasant-enough high school with some nice features and some competent, dedicated, and likeable staff that one could easily and reliably talk with adult-style. Yet it was not to be. From speaking to other glassy-eyed parents, maybe he's just a typical boy. At least until now.

I'm concerned as parents annoyingly are, about Jet returning to the standard fun-filled school milieu. If he's not mature enough and equipped enough to understand exactly how to win friends, teachers, and influence people, and thus to get the best out of an often needlessly flawed system that nonetheless does have many talented teachers in it, he may just as likely go back rather quickly to how he was just four months ago. And in that hideous case, either Jet leaves home or we do.

Frank's Recollections

The following are Frank's recollections of his early teaching days in 1950, which he recounted to me two years ago, in 2019, when he was 90 years old.

Sam and his Gig

After a lapse of seventy years, I can comment on the Christian Brothers who taught me. I am an experienced teacher of boys (and sometimes girls) from prep to year twelve. The Christian Brothers certainly got a bad press. A small fraction of the Christian Brothers were homosexual and of these I remember only one as being an unpleasant nuisance, who was (according to the school grapevine) expelled. Anyhow, he vanished. The rest were excellent teachers.

I had received the English prize in year eleven, which I hope still shows in my writing. This was ignored by St Kevin's principal, a forbidding autocrat nicknamed Soccer – definitely no sporting reference intended – who decided that I was to become a maths/science student. This was like an edict from the Holy Ghost and no negotiation was entered into. Toward the year's end, I panicked, read the English Literature books and put my name in for the exam – fortunately I passed it and Soccer's two subjects. So, I matriculated; I could enrol at Melbourne University, but I didn't. I eventually enrolled at Melbourne Teachers' College, which was staffed by very experienced grade six teachers with hard-earned degrees.

As I had matriculation, I put my name down for a year of teacher training. First, though, I had to do a year's apprenticeship at a local primary school – Glen Iris. The principal was Bill Eddy. Bill (definitely don't call me Bill) was another autocrat. Not quite the same brand as Soccer Saul at St Kevin's, but cast in the same mould. His qualifications were all the gift of the old Victorian Education Department, and he earned them all and policed them when his teachers applied for them. He addressed me by my surname, which was a novelty to my seventeen-year-old self, and demanded performance to match. School inspectors and even infant mistresses treated him very warily. I treated him like a pile of radium, but from my present perspective I see him as a very expert and committed principal.

The two variables in academic instruction are reading and numeracy. My practical experience of reading instruction began in the bush, circa 1950, where I taught a four-year-old girl all the sounds that made up *Sam and his Gig*, in the grade one reader. She knew all the sounds but could not synthesise them into Sam or gig or anything else, if it comes to that. This puzzled me. (A gig, incidentally, is a two-wheeled horse-drawn carriage, familiar then to all our fraternity of twenty-year-old bush head teachers. Modern gigs are different and noisier.)

Then one day she got it – the light went on and she happily ploughed through all the phonetically regular words in the grade one reader.

Next week, the inspector came and very reluctantly – he was a good bloke – sent her home to milk the cows. She was too young. I still remember her tired face with sometimes a smear of cow dirt attached.

That first reader was the teaching bible for underpaid but highly efficient infant mistresses. These teachers, who not only governed large staff and large classes but were the authority behind its publication, were widely consulted by the inspectors, but were paid peanuts. I include this to stress that formal arithmetic started in grade three, after two years of reading instruction largely based on phonics. My memory tells me that my grade three classes in the bush and in a housing commission area where I taught, were based on the grade three reader, *Vivid History Reader*, and grade three arithmetic book, but the stress was on reading. The head teacher and inspector judged you on reading, arithmetic, and a mystic aura called "class tone", which I intuitively understood but found difficult to define, yet always quickly recognised when I saw it in a classroom. So, I am simply saying that we had a pretty good reading syllabus in the grade one reader, which was supervised by a group of strong-minded and underpaid spinsters – let's give them some recognition. They sure had mine.

Eventually, I finished up in charge of 120 children and three teachers in a large rural school. By then I felt like a battle-hardened veteran. I had passed the Education Department exams of promotion, two of which were university standard. My inspector mentioned that I could almost certainly receive part-time study-leave on full money to complete a degree. Remember that I had matriculation when a large proportion of my mates who classified as outstanding teachers did not. They had entered teachers' college with a form five leaving certificate. They remained outstanding, but this was a long time ago and that was that – academically, nowhere else to go.

Anyway, in spite of all this, my response was pretty much, "Let's go! Who do I have to shoot?" So started my seven-year academic career, but I stayed the same primary teacher with attitudes imprinted in the old primary division – alas perhaps indelibly imprinted after seventy years on the job. My university degrees simply increased my scepticism. I read the discussions about phonics and think of my very tired four-year-old little girl and her twenty-year-old teacher and our eventual success.

All of the present investigations into reading instruction remind me of the fourteenth century bookmen who deliberated on how many angels can dance on the point of a needle – today's young teachers seem to be getting more than their share of needles to contemplate. ("How many angels can dance on the point of a needle" is a phrase that, when used in modern contexts, can be a metaphor for wasting time debating topics of no practical value or consequence, and is attributed to Thomas Aquinas.)

The Judo Years

A lot had been said about Frank's involvement in judo. He achieved the seventh-dan grading, which was the highest in Australia. Frank was athletic, strong, and of average height when I met him in 1998. Apart from his involvement in judo instruction, which took place anywhere he was asked to go, he religiously carried out his exercise program using the Canadian 5BX program. Every morning, the sound of floorboards thumping could be heard coming from the dojo attached to the house. He also swam at the Monash pool whilst demonstrating stroke development to students, as well as his weekly adult judo classes.

Frank was always doing something – either physical activity or reading from his extensive library. He had held most administrative positions with Judo Australia and was even selected to compete in the Tokyo 1964 Olympics.

His final selection did not take place. Although considered the best, Frank could be obstinate, and if he didn't approve of how things were run, he would not be swayed. Such was his view of Judo Australia at the time. He formed an alternate group; they went to court and Frank's group won and were given a sum of money that Frank used to encourage any future promising judo players. But this was at the price of his inclusion in the Olympic team. His replacement, Peter, a firm friend, still says today that Frank was the number one player.

I recently read the New South Wales history of judo, and one page tells the story of a competition with the best players in New South Wales and the comment there was, "… then we heard the dreaded Frank Dando was coming up."

Frank was the grading secretary of Judo Victoria when I met him. Divisions within the association had healed over time. The secretary of Judo Victoria often visited our home; in fact, every second day, as he was Frank's best friend. Bob had been a plumber and a judo player when Frank first met him. Frank persuaded Bob to do an education degree, and he then became a teacher at a technical school and finally at Frank's school, but was by that time seventy and retired.

I learned later that Frank had assisted no less than ten other judo players, mainly tradies, to study and successfully become teachers. He didn't just stop at their enrolment, but assisted them with their research. One such person, John Deakin from Tasmania, came up to me at Frank's funeral – quite a distance to travel, but such was the respect that is also a tenet of the judo ethic. Continuing his love of teaching and furthering others, he encouraged the present Academy principal, Zak, to complete a master's degree. This was when I first began at the school. Fortunately for me, I already had two degrees, and anyway, I was a lot older than these younger men.

As Bob was secretary of Judo, it was his job to award the grading certificates and as I had some calligraphy skills, I offered to write them out and keep the records. Thus, I became more ensconced in the judo life. I attended tournaments and watched the competitors with interest.

The school students became proficient as they practised under Frank's tutelage three days each week. Once a year, the thirty students would all pile into the school's Toyota bus and head off down the highway to Geelong. There, they would be part of the Kardinia International College tournament. The physical education teacher there, Doug Noak, was a judo player and the school was affiliated with Japan, the home of judo. Interested surrounding schools that had judo in their curriculum were our competitors, such as Bendigo and Ballarat. Our school always came second; Kardinia, with Doug at the helm and larger student numbers, always won.

It was interesting to see non-judo players from the school pile into the gym at lunchtime, and I remember the girls in their long, green, tartan skirts cheering their school on. The gymnasium had three soft judo mats and each had two referees. Many of our parents drove down and were in the stands cheering on our students. One noticeable difference was the fitness of our students. Many did not have more than a year's judo training due to the two-year tuition period at our school, but they were super fit because of the daily physical education and swimming. Once they had a good hold, there was every chance they would win.

We had been invited to Hobart for the Australasian Martial Arts Hall of Fame awards night, where there would be demonstrations of various martial arts and a gala awards night. Frank had been asked to dress formally in a black-tie tuxedo. The function was held at the Wrest Point Hotel Casino. Soon, people arrived from all over Australia and some from New Zealand. The dressed-up ladies and men were an eye-catching spectacle, as was the evening's entertainment.

Young students of taekwondo and aikido gave a display, then came a Chinese drum performance, followed by the Chinese community presenting a wonderful selection of their colourful dragons. Frank was asked to lead the dragons as a dragon master, and although reticent, he had the stick thrust into his hands and led the dragons throughout the tables of diners. Later in the evening, Frank was awarded the Leading Sensei of Judo and also a Legend of the Martial Arts. Before they announced Frank's name, Tino Ceberano was speaking on the podium. He noticed Frank in the crowd and immediately changed his speech to include how Frank had been his sensei in earlier years. It was quite a feat for Tino and also a mark of respect.

Frank and I continued to attend the annual AMAHOF event and in 2018, an amazing award was given. Leading athletes from various disciplines and countries received awards, then they announced that some non-martial artists had contributed largely to the effectiveness of judo. I could hardly believe it when they called me up to the podium to receive this award. I received a framed certificate and a trophy, which I have on the wall of the family home in Warburton.

To cap the evening off, I even won the raffle, which was a superbly crafted quilt!

This year, 2023, I will again attend the AMAHOF, which will be held in Sydney where they are planning to have a tribute to Frank and his many achievements throughout his seventy years in judo.

Skiing

I was sixty when Frank asked me if I wanted to learn to ski. I knew that I had good balance and had played basketball until I was fifty-six, so agreed to give it a go. The first thing I learned was never get coached by your husband or any other skier, especially one more experienced than you, because they never want to stay on the beginners' slope. I joined Frank's group of skiers, even though I was very much the beginner. They called themselves The Rock Splitters. I think the name was meant to sound fearless.

Anyway, we all drove up to the resort at Jindabyne, where we were housed in individual huts but were very comfortable. The next morning, Frank organised the lift tickets and we drove to Bullocks Flat, where we caught the funicular-type train that travelled through the mountain, passing Perisher and Thredbo, and on to Blue Cow, the peak. On the train, there was a cacophony of skier's boots clunking and the rattle of skis being carried for the day's activities.

Frank tried to give me some rudimentary instruction, then left me on top of Blue Cow with an easy slope to practise on, but I should have taken several formal lessons. I used the run that had a rope tow. The rope went up the slope and had to be fished out of the snow, then you held on and were dragged up the slight slope, letting go at the top and snow ploughing down.

We were there for five days and I did eventually find an instructor with a small group. I found I could manage on a green run! I could even turn and stop. After that, Frank and I travelled to Canada where I had more lessons and could manage the chairlift comfortably. Over the years, we skied in many snow fields in America, Canada, Japan, New Zealand, and Australia, and I progressed to managing blue runs but never black. Frank loved to ski and was an expert. Every year, Frank and I went with the FDSA school group to Mount Hotham, where the students would all have a ski lesson with instructors in the morning and practise with Frank and us staff in the afternoons. All of my family learned to ski with Frank. Frank's own grand-children also experienced Frank's military style of teaching as well!

Although Frank was an expert skier, he was not known for his sense of direction, even in the car! He was even worse in a white-out on the snow fields, as demonstrated once in New Zealand.

Our group, consisting of Carol, Ross, Frank, and I, had planned a ski trip to New Zealand. The unlikely destination was Mount Ruapehu, central to the North Island; the area is better known for its hot pools, geysers, boiling mud pools, and other thermal activity – but also boasts the largest ski area in New Zealand.

The plane descended into the small Wellington airport situated on the Rongotai isthmus on reclaimed land. The plan was to hire a car and travel north through the desert road, past Taihape, and on through the picturesque country of Tongariro National Park to the Whakapapa village. This was the closest accommodation to the Mount Ruapehu ski fields.

Once we had settled in, hired our skis, and bought our lift tickets, we drove to the ski field – some twenty minutes drive. Parking in the carpark, we read a sign about the possibility of an earthquake. The signed warned that we were in the area of an active volcano that was overdue for some action, and told what to do should it erupt. Undeterred, we walked to the ski lift where the run was named The Rock Garden – hardly evoking hopes of a smooth ski run.

After a few warm-ups on this easy green run, which did indeed have some rocky areas, we progressed to the blue runs. After a few circuits, we noticed that Frank had not joined us to take the ski lift back up Magic Mountain. We waited for some time, then decided to ski the circuit again and look for him. By now, white mist was swirling around and visibility was poor. It was getting later and colder. Eventually, we went to the Rendezvous Lodge at the top of the mountain, where we had planned to meet if we got separated.

After hot chocolates and much discussion, we debated whether we should call in the ski patrol. Frank was the most experienced skier of our group and had skied for many years all over the world. He had also told us of his many adventures and how once in the Rockies he had skied into a tree. He was knocked unconscious, and remembers the ski patrol hovering over him saying, "Are you alright, Gramps?" He wasn't worried about his head injury, just his pride at being called Gramps.

There were signs up at strategic points saying that skiers going beyond the designated boundaries would incur huge fines. Keeping this in mind, we decided to wait a bit longer before calling in the ski patrol. After we had been there about two hours, Frank and another man we did not recognise staggered in the door. Icicles hung from Frank's beard and moustache, and his grey face showed he was exhausted. After a hot drink and divesting his dripping coat, helmet, goggles, and gloves, he was able to tell us what had happened.

He had noticed an interesting short cut, outside the boundary and of course off-piste. He soon discovered why it was roped off, and the folly of just skiing under the red tape. As he skied past a tree, he sank down in the soft snow into a tree well, up to his shoulders. Frank was deciding how to cope with the situation when another foolish skier joined him. He was an American who later said that if he had to get into that situation, Frank was the best person to do it with. Frank's nature is one of patience and determination. He'd had a lot of experience in the snow, and he kept upright and his airway clear, tamping the soft fluffy snow methodically, until eventually they could crawl out.

After a good night's sleep, the ski holiday continued without any further mishaps and a good time was had by all. It would be good to think that Frank's skiing adventures would not cause any further concerns, but since this incident he has been lost several times, knocked himself out on a rock, and the last time, in 2019, had to have all the ski patrols on Mount Hotham looking for him.

Here is a limerick written by a student in my English class, after the ski camp at Mount Hotham:

James Hindle once went to Mount Hotham,

He said, "I will ski to the bottom."

He put on his skis,

Only then did he see,

Skis don't always go where you want them!

My Art Years

I have always been interested in art, and was teaching my grade five and six class when a new teacher joined the staff. Lenore was appointed coordinator of middle school and I soon struck up a friendship with her. She joined my basketball team, and as I got to know her, I became aware of her considerable drawing skills. She told me she continually drew horses when she was a child, as she was always involved with them around the Yarrambat area where she grew up and still lived.

One day, she invited me to join a plein-air painting group with Joe Attard, a local artist I later came to know through his exhibitions and impressive work. We were to meet in Zig Zag Road, Eltham, and as I drove my small, yellow Gemini along steep unmade roads, I wondered if this was where I wanted to be. I thought my skills were just passable; I had always illustrated my chalk board with whatever theme I was teaching, so thought, *How hard can it be?* Well, I soon found out.

I positioned my borrowed easel beside Lenore, and soon enough Joe began pointing out the salient points of the vista before us. The scenery was lush, looking down on swathes of verdant pastures with stands of gum trees in small groups, and to large, gnarly, mature eucalypts close by. When he began to draw our attention to the "reds and blues in the trees" and explain how "green isn't always green," I began to see that I was out of my depth.

The other artists were all experienced oil painters, and as he went on further to talk about colour and light, foregrounds and distances, and composition – "Don't put your focal point in the centre, use the method of thirds" – I quickly positioned my easel behind Lenore, and as we were sharing her oil paints this was easy. I just tried to copy whatever Lenore was doing. It was a rather tedious session and not at all satisfying.

After this, Lenore suggested I join a group where lessons were taught, and I began where I should have started. I was fortunate to have an excellent tutor named Ron Reynolds. By now, two other staff members joined us – one even venturing into cubism.

The lessons were held in the local Eltham Primary School, and one session we were going to have a life-drawing class, but our model did not turn up. It was a parent-teacher night at the school, and a parent wandered into the art room by mistake. After a friendly chat, where he told us he had finished his interviews, he offered to become our model for the night! I wonder how he discussed the reports to his family.

I had to leave these classes when I enrolled at La Trobe to do a degree in social sciences at night, while teaching full time.

Some years later, after my husband had died, I returned to oil art classes with Karolyn Mitchell, which was a lovely experience. I managed to produce some paintings that I was very happy with, even selling a few and winning a regional art show. I was fortunate to continue painting with Lenore.

Five years after Kevin passed, I married Frank Dando who ran a special school in Ashwood, and I moved over to the other side of Melbourne. The school enrolled students who had failed in the mainstream system but were bright. One student, Karim, came to the school with a history of graffiti. I asked him if he would like to forgo one maths class and come with me to the Malvern Art Society, which was nearby. His parents agreed, as he had some talent at drawing. The medium used here was pastel – a new experience for me.

Karim was very keen and when he arrived, the very middle-class, older, traditional-type ladies asked, "Have you done much painting, dear?"

He replied, "Only on trains."

Needless to say, they were taken aback, but this student was confident and had great personal skills, as well as real ability with art. He often walked around and admired other students' art, offering comments, so they soon warmed to him.

At the end of the term, our teacher explained that the following week we would have a model and do some life drawing. She would provide various positions for quick life sketches. I was a bit nervous and thought, *How can this work? A nude model and an immature teenager.*

On the way back to school, I asked him, "Do you think you are mature enough for this class? It's likely that the lady will be old and have wrinkles. All you have to do is concentrate on your art and measurements."

He assured me all would be fine.

The next week, when we arrived, the usual model – an older lady – wasn't there. Instead, a gorgeous nineteen-year-old model had her dust coat on, ready to begin once we were all settled. I made a quick decision to place my student at the other end of the group, away from me.

The lesson was handled expertly by the art teacher, Regina, of course, and excellent work was done by all. Karim was able to comment on other students' work regarding measurements and light in an expert manner. Art was a changing experience for this student, who progressed well academically, gave up graffiti, and now is an estate agent, married to a doctor. He keeps in touch with the school and recently said, "We must catch up for a coffee."

My painting had progressed and pastel was now my medium of choice, although I still produced some oil paintings.

One of my last paint-outs with Lenore was when my granddaughter was going to Byron Bay for her year twelve schoolies week. She wanted to go, but was a bit nervous about what the group might decide to do. She wasn't keen to stay long hours into the morning in a night club. She asked me if I would like to come, but stay at a discreet distance in a different venue. Lenore and I saw this as an excellent opportunity to paint in this magnificent setting. We only received one friendly call from Ella, who enjoyed her week. We were impressed with the behaviour of students from various schools when we saw them about the town, and especially with the Red Frogs who had set up coffee tents to be available for anyone. We were able to visit Nimbin and the Currumbin Wildlife Sanctuary and paint the ocean in its various moods. We quite liked being able to say we were part of schoolies week.

Janine

Janine is one of those students a teacher always remembers. I first met her as a grade two teacher, then as the Aust Swim examiner when I was testing all of the grade six students.

The first time I met Janine, she came into my grade two classroom – a tall, blonde girl with a serious face. She asked, "Can I borrow a harder reading book? I like to read chapter books."

She had been sent by her grade one teacher, Lyn Ansell, as she had read all of the suitable books in the grade one library. We moved over to the book case and I asked, "Do you have any favourite authors?"

She replied, "I like to read Roald Dahl books."

I selected *Fantastic Mr. Fox* and *James and the Giant Peach*. When she stretched out her arm to take them, I could see a glint of metal. Two prongs of silver separated to clutch the books. I stood frozen to the spot, then realised that here was this child from grade one behaving quite normally, and here was I showing my shocked reaction. I quickly gathered my thoughts and made a remark about what a good reader she was for a grade one person, and told her I also loved reading.

"Come back any time; just let me know what you are borrowing."

It was five years later that I encountered Janine again. I was at the Thomastown public swimming pool and I was examining students for their junior swimming certificates. I had just finished testing a large grade six girl, Angela, who had swum confidently and easily passed all of her tests. Angela asked, "Can I practise my swimming in the diving pool while you are testing the others?"

As there were already some students there, I confidently agreed saying, "You should be quite safe as you swam very well in your test."

After a loud splash, which was Angela jumping in, I glanced over to see her submerging quickly. In a few seconds she was on the bottom of the diving pool – and stayed there! Panic set in! About twenty possibilities flashed through my mind. *Was there a floatation aid about? Did I have a reach stick?* And then, *would I have to dive the four metres to the bottom?*

Quietly, a head popped up from below the water at the edge. It was Janine – now a grade six student. She asked, "Would you like me to get her for you Mrs J?" Not waiting for an answer, Janine, with one good arm and the other finishing just above the elbow, dived straight down and surfaced holding the shoulder strap of Angela's bathers. Other students helped propel Angela to the edge. By this time Angela's grade six teacher, Mr Nicolas, had arrived at the pool edge and took over. He coaxed Angela back into the regular pool to regain her confidence.

On the bus going back to school, I sat next to Janine and thanked her for her timely assistance. She asked me if she could join my lunchtime basketball team and of course I agreed. Janine displayed above-average athletic skills. She used both arms competently and was an asset to the team, but it was her attitude, drive, and personality that impressed me. She told me that she was a thalidomide child and needed her prothesis adjusted every year, but she never concentrated on her disability. Janine went on to play competition basketball and her team often played against mine at the Coburg basketball stadium, many years after she had left school.

AMAHOF

AMAHOF is the Australasian Martial Arts Hall of Fame, which is held annually and is run by martial artists, for martial artists, who have achieved the highest grades and experiences, with an ethical perspective. Achievement and recognition is for any gender or age. It does not get involved in the politics between individuals or organisations.

Since Frank's induction in 2006, we have attended each year and the first spouse award was given to me in 2018. This year, in 2023, the event was held in Sydney and 350 people attended from all over Australia and New Zealand. Frank had passed away a few months before and he was to be remembered at this years meeting, so I went.

Each year, on the Friday night, various groups of elite martial artists attended a dinner and mixed and chatted in the spirit of friendship, many having met at various competitions during the year.

Saturday, from 7.30 in the morning, martial artists from many disciplines, including Muay Thai, kickboxing, judo, aikido, kendo, and taekwondo, gathered in the ballroom of the Catholic Club, next to the large new Mercure complex in Liverpool, Sydney. All gathered to see demonstrations of techniques with martial artists in full dress of Gi with appropriately graded belts (they were all black belts or dan-graded red and white). Some outfits featured ballooning trousers and the owners carried a ceremonial sword that hung at their side in a gilded scabbard – very fierce looking. After a brief session watching, I usually visited a local shopping centre to spend the rest of my day, leaving the martial artists and Frank to it.

On Saturday evening, there was a gala event where all were dressed formally – men in tuxedos and women in formal gowns, which made for a very sparkly affair. During the meal, which was spread out from 6 to 10 pm, there was entertainment and the inductees were introduced and received their awards. The award was a ring with an impressive large stone fitted well due to size information previously obtained. There was also a wall plaque with the appropriate levels of achievement.

As each inductee came to the podium, they outlined the most significant aspect of their club or their own experiences. Most described the discipline and persistence required to achieve their goals, and praised their mentors. They spoke of their own adult classes, as well as many junior organisations in clubs and schools, saying children gained not only fitness, health, and skill, but that the ethos of fair play and respect was also engendered. I could see this demonstrated in the greeting of a small bow given and had observed this at all junior tournaments. One comment that rang true was, "If it comes too easy, it isn't worth having."

During the evening, there was one speech from an inductee that really struck a chord with me. This man began training in martial arts from the age of three under the watchful eye of his father. An Australian-born Chinese man from Brisbane, he currently teaches tai chi, supporting people suffering neurological degenerative diseases as well as Parkinson's. His speech went as follows:

> I was walking down a city street in Hobart and it was just beginning to get dark. I was holding the hand of my four-year-old son. I could feel someone walking behind me. As the man got closer, I moved to one side, hoping he would pass. He wore a very raggedy, dirty coat, and had a dishevelled

appearance. He stopped beside me and was about to speak when I said, "I don't have any money. I do not carry cash," and brushed him aside.

He just stayed there and as we walked on, my son said, "What did the man want? You never let him speak."

I began to think about this. My four-year-old would remember this encounter. I was not setting a very good example.

I stopped and said, "Let's see if we can find him."

So, we walked back and found the man. I said to him, "I'm sorry I didn't find out what it was you wanted and never gave you the time to speak."

The man said, "I just wanted some spare change to catch the bus."

I then said, "I really do not carry cash, so I can't give it to you."

The man's demeaner was now very uplifted and I could see that he was feeling good that I had afforded him the opportunity to speak.

The lesson I learned was that everyone deserves some dignity, no matter what the circumstances. I felt that I had passed on a very valuable contribution.

For my part, I was impressed with the way the inductee delivered his story and it is the one I remember from the evening.

My Three Children

Wayne

My first child Wayne was born in the 1950s when I was seventeen. Luckily, I had married into a supportive family, as I was a fairly naïve girl from the bush. When Wayne was born, I had little experience with babies and the Queen Victoria Hospital decided I should remain at the hospital for three weeks. It was normal at those times to stay in hospital for one week, but three weeks seemed never-ending. Wayne had to be fed with a bottle and the formula used was condensed milk with drops of vitamins, like Pentavite, added. Eventually, my husband Kevin signed me out of the hospital with the purpose to take the baby to the local health centre once a week. Wayne thrived and was a happy baby; he was easy to look after. A nappy-wash service supplied three-dozen cloth nappies twice a week. Soiled nappies were placed in a large metal bin.

We lived in a bungalow at the rear of the owners' house, so it wasn't long before I got a job (much to Kevin's dislike), and my sister-in-law looked after Wayne. Wayne grew into a quiet boy – very pleasant and compliant. He joined the local youth club and participated in sports, such as football and cricket. Wayne wasn't an exceptional scholar and his reading was quite poor when he was in grade four.

One evening, there was a knock at the door and I could see a salesman on the porch. As I was cooking the evening meal, my husband was selected "to get rid of him." Kevin was gone for a long time and I went to see what was keeping him, just in time to see him finish signing off on a contract to buy a set of *Newnes Pictorial Encyclopedias*. When the twelve-volume encyclopedia set was delivered a few days later, it was quite impressive. As well as lots of written information, all easily referenced with a table of contents and an index, there were coloured transparent overlays. Sections of animals and humans could be built up by turning the next transparent page over the previous one. This set of factual information fascinated Wayne, who would regularly take them out and read them. Thus, his reading improved dramatically and perhaps pointed to his later vocation.

Every morning the boy next door, Chris Skeggs, would stop at our front gate and call out in a crow-like voice, "Wa-ayne," and Wayne would go out to join him for the three-kilometre walk to Keon Park Technical School. It was the early 1970s and teachers were in short supply. In the secondary system, anyone who had any sort of academic background could become a teacher. Wayne's English teacher had a very heavy accent and even I couldn't understand him at parent information nights.

Kevin and I decided Wayne should leave at the end of year ten and learn a trade. He became an apprentice lift mechanic. In those times, parents were very involved in selection of trades. We went along to the interview with Wayne and signed off on his indenture. Wayne spent four days on the job and one day each week studying at RMIT. He would be assigned to a qualified electrical mechanic for the four working days each week.

One mechanic he was assigned to was a TV character from the Mickey Mouse show. As well as singing the theme song – "M-I-C, K-E-Y, M-O-U-S-E" – he could throw his voice and make it sound like it was coming from a grate in the street. Another employee was a train spotter, and they would travel all over Melbourne to watch the trains going under bridges. The worst one was a man who would stop the lift and have a sleep. Such was the life of an apprentice!

Around this time, Wayne became interested in baseball. He was not an exceptional player, but became a very good coach of juniors, taking Preston to be premiers over the famous and never-beaten Red Legs of Waverley. He spent a lot of time coaching and even billeted some interstate players at our house. Wayne gave 100% to everything he put his mind to, practising and reading any information he could find. He became the Victorian junior league coach, and an expert in the dynamics of pitching. He was still a quiet person, but won an award from Prime Minister Howard for his service to junior sport.

Wayne eventually left the lift mechanic job after he had qualified, and he worked as an electrical mechanic in a position where he became interested in the use of polymer; Australia, along with Germany, was the first country to use polymer for the composition of their money. Although he'd achieved formal education to year ten, Wayne began to work as a scientist and has written articles published in science magazines. Wayne has never married but is a close uncle to his nieces, and the rest of his family.

Michelle

Michelle was born four years after Wayne, and I was a much more experienced mother by this time. We were out of hospital in six days and had no setbacks. I went back to work, as we had just bought our first house and Kevin had broken the tibia and fibula in his leg. Michelle was always a delightful child. She was very outgoing and her experiences at Burbank Primary School and Lalor Technical School were happy ones.

We had very different expectations for Michelle, who firstly became a primary school teacher, but found in 1982 it was difficult to get a permanent position. An advertisement in the newspaper said that there was a shortage of mathematics and science teachers in the secondary system. The advertisement was for teachers with a mathematics background to teach in country areas. The idea was that they teach three days each week and study at Deakin University two days.

Michelle was not keen to go to the country and considered the potential areas of Mildura and Orbost much too far to go. As I glanced through the country areas, I noticed Sunbury was listed. This was only half an hours drive from our house in Reservoir, and so she moved to a position there teaching year twelve English, as well as maths and geography, in her first year. She loved this school and settled in to become a maths, science, and geography teacher.

Michelle was a very good basketball player and while at high school played in my team of adults with the local youth club. Although only 1.52 metres tall, she could do a very handy lay-up. She also played in the school team and got on well with the physical education teacher, Kay Edwards. Kay was coaching the school technical team to compete in America. Michelle was asked to train with them, but we thought at Michelle's height there was no way she would be in the team. Costs and booking air fares were discussed, which we were not in a position to consider, and anyway her height would preclude her – or so we thought. She came home after the final selection was made and told us she could be included in the team. We said there was no way we could afford it, and to her credit she did not complain. I always regretted that she did not go.

Michelle taught for the next ten years, got married, and has two lovely girls – Ella and Sian.

After having Sian, Michelle has been involved with helping her husband in his town planning business in South Melbourne. Michelle has many talents. She can copy and sew most things, cooks signature dishes, and recently reupholstered her dining chairs – and mine!

Nine years after Michelle arrived in our family, and fourteen years after having Wayne, we decided to have another child.

Some months later, in 1970, when we found our wishes had come true, we were confident that all would be well – or so we thought! I continued to work at the office as well as volunteer, teaching balancing beam gymnastics at the local youth club. As I was also treasurer, I was present to collect the fees for various activities every Wednesday night.

I went for my six-month check-up at PANCH Hospital and was told that all was well. Working in an office as a sales estimator at my desk the next day, I developed severe pains in my back and knew there were likely to be serious problems, as I was only six months pregnant. After seeing the doctor, I drove myself to the PANCH Hospital and baby Michael was born within the hour. Unfortunately, he weighed only two pounds. He was perfectly formed – even a bit rounded – but was struggling to breathe in an intensive-care incubator. He was just too premature and lived for only one day. He had to be named, birth registered, and my husband had to arrange a funeral. We also received the baby bonus from the government, which was automatically given for all babies born at that time.

This was a huge blow for our family and difficult to cope with. I began to keep the two children, Wayne and Michelle, home from school to be with me. But I knew that I needed to return to work.

Kevin

One year later, we had our next child. This time I left work early, gave up my duties at the youth club, and tried to be as careful as possible. We had some private health insurance so I became a private patient. This baby was also premature, but just reached seven months and weighed 4 pounds, 11 ounces.

It was quite frightening seeing him in intensive care with his little chest labouring up and down, struggling for breath. He had to be gavage fed, which meant a tube going through his nose straight to his stomach. A paediatrician visited him every day at the private hospital in Coburg. We wondered how we were ever to cover this extra cost. Still, we decided whatever happened we still had our baby. Another patient at the hospital told us she had taken out a loan with Custom Credit to cover her unexpected costs. Our insurer worked with us and we managed the costs through them.

With a mass of white-blond hair, baby Kevin arrived home after two months. Although he was slower to reach some milestones, Kevin thrived. He was spoilt by everyone and was an alert and very bright child. He had excellent teachers in the early primary school years and was an avid reader. By grade four he was reading *The Hobbit* and the set of *The Lord of the Rings*. He liked to read everything – even the labels on sauce bottles on the table.

Kevin began school at four and a half years of age. His birthday was 6 June, and the end of June was the cut-off date. If a child turned five by the end of June in the year they commenced, they could be enrolled. The primary school years were enjoyable ones with Michelle at Lalor Technical School and Wayne working as an apprentice. Whilst at primary school, Kevin loved to compose jokes and I remember one he liked to tell when he was in grade four. He said:

> Mr Bob Hawke and Mr Malcolm Frazer were on a balcony watching a political demonstration. Mr Bob Hawke said, "I think I will throw 1000 dollars out and make 1000 people happy."
>
> Mr Malcolm Frazer said, "I will throw 5000 out and make 5000 people happy."
>
> Mr Bob Hawke said, "I will throw you out and make everybody happy."

Kevin played the flute and we were looking for a suitable high school for him, out of our Reservoir area. MacLeod High was a music school, and one of his friends was going there as well.

He struggled socially at the beginning of year seven. Just when we thought we should move him back to Reservoir with most of his other friends, he settled in and achieved excellent results.

In grade six, he had won a place at Ivanhoe Grammar for boys, but needed to sit a maths test. It was a cold, frosty morning when we arrived at Ivanhoe Grammar for Kevin to sit the exam; cold enough to see the steam coming from our breath. The master came out to address the boys assembled in front of him. He was dressed in black academic robes and carried some sort of stick in his hands. He exuded authority. This was my impression and I began to think this was a mistake. He turned to the students and led them inside saying, "Now boys, come with me."

Kevin achieved a very high score and they kept Kevin's place open for three years, but we decided on Macleod High with its musical history. Kevin never did play his flute at that school, but he was involved in their drama activities, playing a part in *Singin' in the Rain*. At Macleod, Kevin formed a good friendship group whom he still sees today. They were a group of boys and one girl – Jenny. They played indoor cricket and the game *Dungeons and Dragons* at each other's homes. Kevin even wrote some of the games.

Although Kevin's English was excellent – he even wrote a short story in year ten, titled "The Fortune" – he decided to try for a career in engineering. In year twelve, he sat the maths, physics, chemistry, and English subjects and received an ATAR of 96. Such was his determination that when he finished the maths B exam, he felt he had not done so well, so he contacted the physics teacher and asked for some extra tuition to boost his physics. There was a four-day period before the exam, and I drove him to Doncaster the three nights to have time with his physics teacher. Credit should also go to the teacher for giving him the extra time.

With his high ATAR, Kevin was able to pursue his chosen career of aeronautical engineering. He went on to do a master's degree by research and spent many hours in a "cell" in Port Melbourne testing fatigue factors on skin structures of aircraft. A previous student had left a gun that fired chickens at engines of aircrafts for his studies. Kevin modified the gun to fire ice balls at the aircraft structures. He made the hailstones and recorded the results usingAutoCAD on the computer. This technology was very new and innovative in the early nineties. Whilst studying, he was chosen to join a research company and still works for them today.

Kevin's English has always been outstanding, so I decided to include this short story Kevin wrote when he was sixteen years old for a year ten assignment.

Kevin lives in Fairfield in a weatherboard Edwardian house that he has almost finished renovating.

"The Fortune" by Kevin

> The carnival had always been one of Eric's favourite spots, so it was the obvious place to go when he had come into money at the races and wanted to celebrate with friends. Presently he was with two of his best friends, Peter and Peter's wife, Jane. Actually, it had been Peter's idea to visit the carnival after the races and Eric considered it a splendid one.
>
> That night the carnival was a swarm of faces, noises, and exotic odours. As the small group walked through the narrow pathways and alleys, they passed dozens upon dozens of stalls and brightly lit caravans selling donuts, hot dogs, or ice-creams. Some sold food of a more exotic nature, such as kebabs, souvlakis, or dim sims. There were the inevitable rides, shooting galleries, a hall of mirrors, wax works, and show-bag stands.

Occasionally, a sign would catch one's eye and interest. Such was the sign that fascinated Peter: Madame Latrouseur – Tarot readings and predictions. Eric laughed cynically when Jane suggested they go and have their fortunes told. But he was in a good mood and agreed to her idea. From outside, the pavilion looked similar to those surrounding it. A dark coloured flap gave entrance to the tent, and as the three pulled it back and stepped in, it was as if they had entered a different world.

As their eyes grew used to the poor light, they saw that they were standing in a small room; its walls were draped with dark tapestries depicting arcane scenes. A mass of silken cushions carpeted the floor and the dim illumination was due to a small candle burning in a perforated brass globe, hanging from the tent's ceiling. On a small table to the left of the entrance was a candle of incense, sending its acrid smoke through the small enclosure. Sitting behind a low table in the centre of the room was a dark-haired woman robed in black silk. Her hair was mostly covered by a triangle of red cloth and on the table in front of her was all manner of equipment relating to the mystic and arcane.

She looked up and smiled at the visitors.

"Welcome! Welcome!" she exclaimed. "Please make yourselves comfortable."

Peter stepped forward. "I was wondering if you would predict our future for us."

"Of course, of course," she said. "Do you mind me using the Tarot?"

"You can use whatever you want," Eric put in. "It won't make any difference."

"Ah!" she declared. "A critic. No," she reconsidered, "a challenge!"

The three seated themselves and Jane offered to be examined first. The procedure was much as they expected. A lot of humming and general predictions that would probably occur to 90% of the world's female population. All throughout the reading, Eric had been on the point of hysterics, giggling and rolling his eyes as each prediction was made.

When the first reading was over, the fortune teller looked mischievously at Eric.

"You really think it's all a game?" she whispered. "You think it's all a joke?"

"What should I think, lady?" Eric laughed. "Should I take it seriously?"

"Yes, I believe you should," she continued in her quiet, almost dangerous voice. "But, to prove my point, how about a little bet?"

"What?" Eric asked, startled.

"Sure," she said. "You write three questions and answers about yourself, which you think I could not possibly know. You put down a thousand dollars and I put down five hundred. If I answer correctly, the money is mine. If I do not, it's yours."

Peter looked interested. "Go on, Eric," he encouraged. "It's easy money."

Eric looked unsure. "But it would mean all of today's winnings gone."

"No worries, mate. You saw what it was like with Jane, Eric. I'll even put in 100 dollars myself and you know how skint I am."

"Alright," agreed Eric. "It's a bet. But what are the questions?" Peter stood up.

"Just write your birthday, parent's names and, say, the colour of your car."

"OK," agreed Eric. "She couldn't get all of them."

"Right," nodded Jane. "How could she?"

The woman clapped her hands.

"Right, Sir, if you could write the answer to your questions on this sheet of paper," she said, handing him a pen and notebook. "We'll put it and the cash on the table."

This was done and the woman nodded in satisfaction.

"Good, good. Shall we begin?"

She leaned back on the cushions and seemed to go into a trance. For five minutes she said nothing, then her eyes sprang open and she took her tarot cards and drew them in four lines of four studying them intently. She repeated the process then finally relaxed. "Well, well," she started. "Would the lady please pick up the paper with the answers on it?"

Jane did so.

"You, Eric Watson, were born of July fifth, 1992." Eric jumped up, startled, with a look of shock on his face.

"Your father was Len Watson and your mother, Irene Smith."

Shock turned to horror and a sweat broke out on his face.

"Your car is black."

Eric sat in shocked silence staring down at the cards, appalled. Peter pushed the money toward her slowly and helped his friend from the tent, followed by an equally bemused Jane.

Fifteen minutes later, Peter knocked on the door of a small caravan on the edge of the carnival grounds. Moments later, the door opened and the dark-haired fortune teller stood in the doorway.

"Oh! It's you, is it?" she said, lighting up a cigarette and adjusting her hairnet. "Your plan worked well. I don't think he suspected a thing." She took out a roll of cash from her pocket, and handed it to Peter.

"There you go. Here's your hundred, plus half your friend's money. Goodbye!" she said as she shut the door, leaving Peter counting his money.

All on a Handshake – 1996

It was 1996 and my first husband, Kevin, had died a few months before, when the following incident took place.

My mother's life centred around purchasing property, while my father continued to work long, twelve-hour shifts at a factory. My sister Marian and her family had decided to move north to a warmer climate, as she had continuous chest infections. Marian and her family had settled on a property in Ashford in northern New South Wales. The property was fairly remote, almost on the Queensland border, with the nearest large town being Inverell. After travelling to inspect it, they decided it was too far out and instead bought a property in Inverell. My mother had been following their plans and she then decided the Ashford property could be a good purchase for herself. She was in her eighties and already had five properties, the others all on the outskirts of Melbourne.

This property, Myuna, was on Limestone Road, Ashford, with large boulders across most of the undulating, dry grassland, prompting the family to call it "Tombstone Territory" and my aunt to remark, "Good Heavens, Jean would buy the Haunted Hills if they were for sale."

After it had been purchased, Kevin and I drove up to look at it during the next holiday period we both had. We travelled along a dirt road that had deep valleys with concreted fords at the bottom, covered by a shallow depth of water, but warning of probable future flooding. The house was a very old Queensland type and seemed to teeter on the tall supports that held the house up. It was about three metres high and had wide steps leading up to the veranda and front door. Inside was clean but spartan, with gleaming linoleum on all floors. The kitchen was supplied with water from a tank and was adjacent to the laundry. There was a large hole in the wall that separated the kitchen from the laundry and the agent had explained the last owner had a tenant who had dogs which had gnawed through it.

The Stock and Station Agent in Ashford said there was an older couple with their son who were interested in renting the house, running sheep and cattle on the property, and growing some plants.

We met Jenny and Roy Reagan and their twenty-year-old son. The Reagans were a simple, hardworking couple best described as "salt of the earth" types. They paid a small rent and the property also yielded some lime to a small mining company, so there was enough income to cover the mortgage on the property.

After they had been on the property for about five years, with Jenny selling her plants at the local Sunday market in Inverell and Roy breeding his sheep, Mum received a letter saying the Reagans had to move from the house as it was now unsafe and Jenny was afraid it might collapse in a storm. The Reagans wanted to put up a large shed to move into and asked if they might have first offer if we decided to sell the property. They wanted to eventually buy it for their son. We weren't sure how this arrangement could work, but agreed to their request.

It was a further five years when we had another letter saying their situation had changed. It seemed their daughter, who lived in Broken Hill, had just had her first child and the little girl was severely disabled. They wanted to move to Broken Hill to support their daughter. Their son no longer wanted to live at Myuna without them, so the dilemma was how to compensate them.

At the time, Kevin had just died and my mother was now eighty-nine years old. I decided to take her to Ashford to look at the property and to see the Reagans; I hired a wheelchair and we caught the plane to Sydney, then the train to Armidale, up through the coal mining areas of Werris Creek, Muswellbrook, and Singleton, passing long trains of coal-filled freight. From Armidale, I hired a car and we travelled north to Inverell where my sister lived. From there, it was an hour's drive north to Ashford.

When we arrived at Myuna, I was amazed to see the transformation. Fruit trees grew in rows watered by large, black irrigation pipes, carrying water from the seasonally flowing Reedy Creek. Not far away from the old house, which amazingly was still standing, was the shed the Reagans had built, which had been lined and supplied with power by a generator. A veranda had been built that afforded extra space. Underneath the old house, amongst the tall stilts or supports, there were rows of propagated plants and hanging baskets. Everything was clean and orderly. At the front gate were sheep yards and a race and ramp to drive the sheep onto transports.

After a cup of tea and a chat, we learned the Reagans had spent about roughly thirty thousand dollars on the property. In its original state it would have been considered derelict, but now was a liveable working concern. In view of Mum's age and the remoteness of the property, we decided to sell it. It was far beyond the capacity of the Reagans to buy the property.

I put forward my proposal – The Reagans consult with the Stock and Station Agents and help to sell the property. We would be happy with a modest $100,000, and anything realised above this price would be given to the Reagans. We shook hands and the deal was made – all on a handshake.

Three months later, the property was sold for $132,000. We instructed our conveyancer to transfer the $32,000 to the Reagans, and the deal was completed.

Two years later, I was on a bus trip to Flinders Ranges and Broken Hill. I rang Jenny Reagan and she came and picked me and a friend up, in the same yellow battered ute I had seen at Myuna. She took us to look at the house she had been able to buy. It was an old house in central Broken Hill, and I was not surprised to see it looking very neat with the improvements Roy was making there.

Retirement

In 2021, Frank and I retired from the Fank Dando Sports Academy. Frank was ninety years of age and I was eighty-one. We always loved what we were doing at the school, so working to those ages was not a chore to us. We sold our building to the school and the Academy is continuing with Zak as principal, and most of the same staff.

Frank died in 2023 and I bought a unit in Montmorency, close to the Were Street shops, the station, and my daughter Michelle, and it's where I live today with my toy poodle Lou.

www.ingramcontent.com/pod-product-compliance
Lightning Source LLC
Chambersburg PA
CBHW041143110526
44590CB00027B/4113